Quite
CONTRARY

Yea rather,
blessed are they that hear the word of God,
and keep it.

—*Luke 11:28*

By this author:

Graven Bread:
The Papacy, the Apparitions of Mary, and
the Worship of the Bread of the Altar

Quite Contrary:
A Biblical Reconsideration of
the Apparitions of Mary

Geese in their Hoods:
Selected Writings on Roman Catholicism
by Charles Haddon Spurgeon
compiled & edited by Timothy F. Kauffman

To order additional copies of *Graven Bread* or *Quite Contrary*, or
Geese in their Hoods, use the order forms at the back of this book,
or write to:

White Horse Publications
P.O. Box 2398
Huntsville, AL 35804-2398

or call White Horse Publications directly at

1-800-867-2398

A complete listing of current White Horse Publications titles is
contained at the back of this book.

Third Edition

CONTRARY

A Biblical Reconsideration of the Apparitions of Mary

by Timothy F. Kauffman

White *Horse*
Publications
Huntsville, Alabama, USA

This is dedicated to Jesus Christ:
my Lord, my God, my Master, my Savior.

He rescued me.

Contents

List of Tables

Acknowledgments

I wish to thank the many friends who encouraged me to write this book. They supported me, they read my manuscripts and they found my most embarrassing mistakes before it was time for the final printing. I owe them many more thanks than they realize. When the first edition of *Quite Contrary* was completed, they distributed it to friends and family and then proceeded to compile an even more extensive list of constructive comments to help make the second and third editions even better. It can be said that these friends of mine are wholly responsible for the fact that *Quite Contrary* has ever seen its fourth printing. Without them, I probably would have let this matter rest. I am glad they convinced me otherwise.

Since the initial publication of the first edition of *Quite Contrary* in 1993, I have received a number of comments from Roman Catholics regarding the conclusions stated in this book. Generally, the same issues are brought up by different people over and over again. Because of this, I added an appendix called "The Mythology of Modern Marianism," a critique of the arguments in favor of Marian devotion as exhibited by Roman Catholicism. Whether the argument is for Marian devotion per Luke 1:48, or for Mary's Queenship, or just for the plain "fittingness" of devotion to Mary, the issue is addressed in the appendix. It is not exhaustive, but when coupled with the body of *Quite Contrary*, the whole is greater than the sum of the parts. It seemed a proper addition to this edition of the book. I hope my readers find it helpful.

I owe many thanks to the people who have taken the time to call or write to let me know that this exhausting task has been worth the effort. I once received a letter from a woman in South

Africa who just wanted to write and encourage me after reading only one page from this book. For her, and others like her—and there have been many—I am deeply grateful. They have been the inspiration for me on days when I wasn't sure it was worth it to work on yet another edition.

As you read, you will notice that I refer to other sources rather extensively. The reason for the references is to assure the reader that my conclusions are based on facts, and that the facts were not taken out of context. Whenever I quote a source or make a factual assertion, I give full credit in the footnotes at the bottom of each page. Though I disagree with many of the sources I used, I admire their authors' thoroughness in compiling the information they have. Their devotion makes mine pale in comparison. I doubt that many of them would be pleased to see their work used in this context, but they would likely agree that it was necessary for the purpose of constructing a viable defense of my position. Whenever possible, I have requested permission to quote the sources directly.

In deference to those who have worked diligently to record and publish the many messages of the apparition of Mary at Medjugorje, Bosnia (formerly the Yugoslav Republic) the following credits are given at their request as one of several conditions under which permission to use their material is granted:

> Many of the messages of the apparition of Mary at Medjugorje are taken from the book *Words From Heaven* (as noted in the footnotes), a book containing over 1,000 of Our Lady's messages from Medjugorje, published by St. James Publishing, P.O. Box 380244, Birmingham, AL 35238-0244. Permission to use this material must be received from St. James Publishing. The book is available by writing to St. James Publishing and enclosing $12 for the book, plus $3 for shipping and handling.

FOR INFORMATION ABOUT MEDJUGORJE

> *Caritas of Birmingham*, an organization committed to being a voice for Our Lady, will send you a free newsletter keeping you up-to-date on all the messages and happenings in Medjugorje. This newsletter is read by well over 100,000 people in 65 countries around the world. Many experts, such as Father René Laurentin, use it to help them in their research. To get this free newsletter, write to: CARITAS OF BIRMINGHAM, Box 120, 4647 Highway 280 East, Birmingham, AL 35242.

Preface

IN the time it took me to advance this book from a rough draft into its first edition, two new Marian-related supernatural events were reported: one in the Philippines and the other in Virginia, USA. Since then, even more apparitions and related paranormal activities have come to my attention. In the time it takes for this book to reach your hands, more apparitions will no doubt surface, and I cannot address them all. I have to accept that my ability to address such issues in a timely manner is limited in a forum like this one.

The topic of Marian apparitions is old—more than eight hundred years old. But in spite of its longevity as a religious controversy, the topic is also obsolescent. New information about Marian apparitions becomes dated in a matter of months, or even weeks, as new apparitions are sighted and their messages are recorded. When an apparition is reported, it usually begins by interacting with one or several people in particular, appearing to them regularly and exclusively and providing messages to them on a monthly, weekly or even daily basis. So while it is difficult to keep up with each new apparition, it is also difficult to keep up with each new message an apparition might deliver. Because of this, it is likely that what you now hold in your hands will not contain the most recent information about the most recent apparitions. But what it does contain is something that controversies and religious issues can never outpace: a Biblical response to them. God's Word is both timely and timeless. It cannot wear out, and neither can it lose its applicability. The answers to our most probing questions about the most difficult issues can be found in the Bible. It is the only standard by which we can be assured a proper judgment about our deepest concerns. I recommend reading it either alongside this book, or instead of it.

It will help you more thoroughly, for a greater length of time, and will answer more questions than this book could ever hope to answer.

*   *   *

A small amount of time invested at some local libraries will reveal to you that there are presently in print hundreds of books dealing specifically with the issue of Marian apparitions. Whether they address the long-standing and Church-approved apparitions like those of Fátima, Lourdes and Guadalupe, or the more recent and still unapproved apparitions, like Medjugorje, Conyers and Garabandal, they all take the same position: "Mary is appearing and has something to tell us." Whether you read *The People's Madonna*, about the apparitions in Medjugorje, or *Our Lady of Fátima*, you will find that the authors base their entire evaluation on one premise: "The apparitions are telling us the truth."

But what if they are not telling us the truth? What if they are lying to us? We are instructed in the Bible to test every spirit, regardless of whom we might believe it to be. Even the Holy Spirit is to be tested for His origins, and when He passes the test, He is glorified, and Christ with Him.

It is with this understanding that I now join the ranks of the many people who have authored books about the apparitions of Mary and the many messages that accompany them. But I take a different stand, a Biblical one: "Prove all things; hold fast that which is good."[1] I invite the reader to do the same.

I have read many books on the topic of Marian devotion and apparitions, and always with a healthy sense of skepticism which has led me to the position in which I now find myself. It is this same skepticism that I ask you to have now as you begin to read. This book is wrong until proven right. Test it. Retain what is good. If anything in this book conflicts with what the Bible says, then the Bible is right, and I am wrong. *Always.*

Keep your Bible at hand as you read to check this book for accuracy. Seek Truth. Come to a conclusion based on the Bible. The Bible will address the issue of Marian apparitions and much, much more. You will do well to place your trust in it. It is God's Word, and the final authority on whatever concerns you.

---

[1] 1 Thessalonians 5:21

Prologue

Behold the Lamb of God, which taketh away the sin of the world.

—John 1:29b

YOU are watching television with your family. Your favorite show breaks for a commercial. You hear a soothing kind of music—many voices, but one song. Not harsh. No words. Just voices. Overtly religious, but not offensive. Now you see a priest. He's holding the paten and a wafer of bread in his hand, obviously about to offer it to one of the faithful. He is wearing the standard liturgical vestments: his alb and his stole. You can see trees behind him. It's an outdoor Mass. The congregation rises in honor of this part of the liturgy. A masculine voice joins in with the music and the ceremony. He asks you in a compassionate voice,

"Have you been away?"

Now a child and another priest. This priest is dressed in obviously Jesuit attire—the characteristic black robe. He is sitting down and the child comes nearer. He takes her hands in his. The little girl is about to tell him something. A Confession is in progress. The music continues and the voice comes back to explain:

"Refresh with the Sacrament of Confession."

Back to the first priest, and another child. A picture of innocence. You can't see the priest, but you can see his garments and his outstretched hand. He is offering something to her. A wafer. He places it into her hands, and again the voice returns, explaining:

"Because the moment of Communion is the highest and most sacred moment of your life."

13

Still another child. She has her eyes fixed on the communion bread as it is lowered into her hands. Reverence. The voice returns for the third and last time:

"This is the moment when the living God enters your heart."

The scene climaxes. The singing is louder than before. A message flashes on the screen informing you that if you wish to obtain a free copy of an audio cassette or wish to know more about coming back home, you may inquire at the address displayed on your TV. Write and ask about "The Lamb."[2] It's not too late to come back to the Church. Without words, the voices seem to be telling you so. They are so soothing. They want you to come back to the Sacrament of Confession. They want you to come back to the Sacrament of the Eucharist.

They want you to come back to the Lamb of God.

Who takes away the sin of the world.

The Lamb of God...

...the Lamb of *Mary*.

---

[2] The contents of the commercial transcribed here are the property of Caritas of Birmingham, ©1991 by Caritas of Birmingham. Used by permission

Introduction

Prove all things; hold fast that which is good.
Abstain from all appearance of evil.
—*1 Thessalonians 5:21,22*

THE words you have just read are the content of a 30-second commercial spot entitled, "The Lamb." It is being distributed by an organization called *Caritas of Birmingham*, in Birmingham, Alabama, USA. *Caritas,** a nonprofit organization, has had "The Lamb" aired free of charge as a public service announcement hundreds of times around the country—even on prestigious cable networks such as CNN† and MTV.§ In one edition of the *Caritas* newsletter, several letters were included from new subscribers who had seen the commercial, and they testified to the power of the imagery used. They want to come back to the Catholic Church now. They write to *Caritas* to tell them that the message is working.

But *Caritas* isn't just trying to bring people back to the Eucharist and to the Church. *Caritas* wants to bring them back to Mary, and specifically, to the apparitions of Mary. From the television commercial described in the Prologue, one would never suspect that, but it is true. The whole ministry of *Caritas* has been changed within the last few years from one of bringing the Catholic message to the world, to one of bringing the messages of Mary to the world: "We believe without a doubt that through God's grace and direction, Our Lady has guided Caritas to be a

---

* Caritas is a Latin word meaning "Love"
† CNN-Cable News Network
§ MTV-Music Television

voice for Her messages and to distribute them to this country and to 65 foreign countries as well."[3]

The new main building at *Caritas* is called "The Tabernacle of Our Lady's Messages," the primary purpose of which will be to distribute the messages of the apparition of Mary at Medjugorje, Bosnia to the whole world. The 'Tabernacle' will house several ministries, including the following: BVM (Blessed Virgin Mary) Pilgrimages, OLPGs (Our Lady's Prayer Groups), OIM (Operation Introducing Medjugorje), and the House of Loreto publishing division. Add to these the ministry that circulates the commercial spot entitled "The Lamb." It is called TLM, for "The Lamb of Mary." TLM is the part of *Caritas* that produces audio tapes, video tapes and advertisements for newspapers and other periodicals.[4] TLM is also responsible for more than 6,000 billboards on display in more than 125 cities in the United States. These billboards are seen by millions of people every day, and bear a picture of Mary beckoning her children back to the faith. Back to the Catholic Church. They include a toll-free phone number with an address for people who want more information about coming home. And people are coming back, sometimes after a 40-year absence from the Church.[5] They call and write to *Caritas* to tell them that the billboards are working.

Because of this level of commitment and outreach, *Caritas* has become a highly developed organization, and it is just beginning to achieve the efficiency and professionalism required to build a following of the magnitude they have visualized. And they are serious. In an article devoted entirely to their newfound purpose, they write, "Peace will come through the children of the Queen of Peace, who are birthed and schooled in holiness by Her. We, living in the Caritas Community, have given everything to Our Lady, even our futures... Ours will be an envious position for so many who have worked fruitlessly, through human work and effort, to bring about peace through man. Yet, ours is a path, the unseen spiritual path, which guarantees peace. It will be given

---

[3] "What is Caritas of Birmingham?" A tract explaining the mission of Caritas. Used by permission

[4] *Caritas of Birmingham*, quarterly newsletter, June-October 1992 issue, pg. 18, ©1992 Caritas of Birmingham

[5] *Caritas of Birmingham*, January-April 1991 issue, pg. 23. Used by permission

through Our Lady, as a gift from God in reward for our prayers and sacrifices in response to Her call."[6] This deep commitment by the people of *Caritas* sets the standard for other organizations in its class. And there are many.

At present, there are seemingly unnumbered incidents of an apparition identifying itself as the Blessed Virgin Mary and calling all who can hear to conversion. Calling them back to the Catholic Church. And wherever an apparition occurs, there also forms a group of followers who want to do exactly what *Caritas* is doing. They are receiving messages from the apparition of Mary and are being instructed by the apparition to circulate the messages as widely and in as many languages as possible, whether it is in Conyers, Georgia or El Cajas, Ecuador; Phoenix, Arizona or Akita, Japan; Rwanda, Africa, or Lubbock, Texas; San Nicolás, Argentina or Betania, Venezuela; Denver, Colorado or Naju, South Korea. The list goes on and on. The fact is that 232 separate incidents of the apparition have been reported in thirty-two different countries between 1923 and 1975,[7] and well over three hundred since then.[8]

And while the apparitions continue to multiply, the faithful who listen to them continue to fulfill their responsibility to distribute and translate the messages. The world continues to be bombarded by these visits from Heaven, and we have become too amazed with the messages, too caught up in the prophecies, too fascinated by the miracles, and too enamored of the apparitions to ask ourselves, *"Why?"*

It's time that we did.

---

[6] *Caritas of Birmingham*, June-October 1992 issue, pg. 14. Used by permission

[7] *Our Lady Queen of Peace*, "Apparitions of Mary Throughout the World," Special Edition I, 2nd Printing, Winter 1992, Dr. Thomas Petrisko, ed. Pittsburgh Center for Peace, McKees Rocks, PA, 15136, pg. 1. Used by permission

[8] Macfarlane, Bud, Sr., M.I., of the Mary Foundation, in his speech entitled, "Marian Apparitions Explained," recorded on May 18, 1991 at St. Leo's Catholic Church, Elmwood, NJ

Part I Ave Maria

Hail Mary, full of grace, the Lord is with thee; blessed art thou among women, and blessed is the Fruit of thy womb, Jesus. Holy Mary, Mother of God, pray for us sinners, now and at the hour of our death. Amen.

—*The Hail Mary*

Foundations

And [I] profited in the Jews' religion above many
my equals in mine own nation, being more
exceedingly zealous of the traditions of my fathers.
—*Galatians 1:14*

IT is difficult to do what I am about to do because it puts me
in an awkward position. Addressing the issue of the
apparitions of Mary is one task, but proving that I have the
authority to do so is quite another. With no seminary training
whatsoever, and no post-graduate studies in Marian devotion at
all, the basis for the ideas put forth in this book would appear to
be poorly founded at best. But I have something that all the
academic training in the world could not replace: a former zealous
devotion to the apparitions of Mary. Years of advanced training
about Marian devotion could never match what I learned from
those years of praying to Mary and honoring all of the
apparition's requests. Clearly I have abandoned this devotion and
have found something new. That much can be said in one
sentence. But I wish to do more than explain that I no longer
follow the apparitions of Mary—I wish to explain why.

This book was written with one thing in mind: to demonstrate
from a Biblical perspective that the apparitions of Mary are not
whom they claim to be. If that assertion can be supported, it
follows naturally that I should wish to warn people to stay away
from them and advise them to ignore the persistent cries for
conversion. Such are my intentions and I wish to be clear about
them from the start. And I believe that my position can be
defended irrespective of my Catholic past. But if I refrain from
relating my Catholic heritage, my former devotion to the Blessed
Mother, my long nights of praying the Rosary and my early
mornings at Mass when I visited the monastery, then you could

easily presume that I was writing from the standpoint of
ignorance. If I refrain from describing my Catholic roots I give
you an excellent reason not to read any further, because for all
you know I may not be capable of comprehending the depths of
the spiritual manifestations I am about to address.

However, the opposite approach can be equally counter-
productive. If I do explain that I used to be Catholic, and have
since trusted Christ as my savior and left the Roman Catholic
Church, then you could easily presume that I am a resentful,
fallen-away Catholic who has a personal vendetta against the
Roman Church. If I tell you that I used to be Catholic but am no
more I give you the perfect excuse not to read any further,
because for all you know I may be writing out of vengeance—and
that if I understood half of what I claimed to, I would still be a
faithful member of the Church.

Either way, I give you a reason to drop the book and walk
away, which of course makes both options equally unattractive to
me. But in order to explain effectively why I have come to this
point I will recount my past, as it weighs heavily in the discussion
on which we are about to embark. But before doing so, I will ask
a favor of the reader. Having been up front about the purpose of
this book, I wish to assure the reader that I have only written that
which is factual and has been documented. And further, regarding
references which describe events accompanying the many and
frequent visions of Mary, I have only quoted from sources
supporting the authenticity of the apparitions, and from the Bible.
Again, my assurance to the reader is that I have only quoted from
sources that acknowledge the authenticity of the apparitions. In
return I ask that you read up to the point that you feel that I have
violated this promise. And if in reading this you arrive at the
conclusion that I am interfering with your personal relationship
with God through Jesus Christ, please discard the book and never
return to it. It is not my intention to harm the Body of Christ, but
to build it up.

With that in mind, I ask you to proceed with a certain
skeptical caution. This is a serious investigation into a serious
supernatural manifestation and I do not desire to imply in any way
that I have taken the issue lightly. Likewise, I do not wish to leave
the impression that I write from an ignorant perspective. So if you
feel it is important to know how I came to believe in the
apparitions of Mary, and subsequently how I turned away from
them, then you may find the rest of this chapter interesting.

I was born in June of 1965 at Balboa Naval Hospital in San Diego, California, USA to Francis Michael and Gayna Carolyn Kauffman. Two weeks later I was baptized into the Catholic Church as Timothy Francis, and very soon after that my father was stationed at the Kaneohe Bay Marine Corps Air Station on the Island of Oahu, Hawaii. We remained there for five years and of course I have no memory of church during that time. I do, however, remember moving back to the mainland in 1970 and I suspect that our church participation in Hawaii must have been as regular as it was when we settled in California.

Upon arriving in Carlsbad, a city on the coast of southern California, I was old enough to enroll in kindergarten, and for my first year of education I attended Jefferson Elementary School because St. Patrick's Catholic Elementary did not have a kindergarten class. When I finally did 'graduate' from Jefferson, I spent the next three years at St. Patrick's, and if memory serves me, we attended church every Sunday morning at St. Patrick's Catholic Church nearby. Occasionally, we drove over the mountain to attend 'the Mission,' but at that age I had no concept of where it was or why it was called 'the Mission,' but I do remember taking the San Luis Rey Road to get there, and I do remember attending Church every Sunday regardless of which church it was. Ours was a devout Catholic family and our neighbors and fellow church-goers knew it well.

My father was soon stationed in Worcester, Massachusetts at a Marine Corps Reserve office there. Because of over-enrollment at the local Catholic parochial school, I spent my first few months at May Street Elementary, a public school. Aside from that, I spent the remainder of my grammar school education at Our Lady of the Angels Elementary, and when our family wasn't attending Mass at Blessed Sacrament Catholic Church on Pleasant Street, it was usually because we had gone to Our Lady of the Angels Catholic Church on Main. It was at Our Lady of the Angels that I first participated in the Sacrament of Confession and at Blessed Sacrament that I received my First Holy Communion. Our family's participation in Mass was as rigorous as our participation in the sacraments, and the few times that we actually missed a service, it was only because we would have been very late or because I was pretending to be sick enough to stay home.

It was at Blessed Sacrament that I first served as an altar boy, a service which I would perform at every church I attended from then on until college. As a family, we participated in church bazaars, blood drives, and brought the bread and wine to the altar occasionally, too. Once, during the Feast of the Coronation of Mary, one of my older sisters was chosen to place a garland of flowers on the statue of Our Lady which was located on the front lawn of the church. We were a devout Catholic family, and if our attendance and participation didn't show it, the size of our family did: we had seven children in the family, and with the exception of the oldest, all of us were born two years apart or less. Among them, I am the fifth.

Although the years we spent at Blessed Sacrament and Our Lady of the Angels Catholic churches in Worcester were not particularly exceptional, one event that took place would affect me for the rest of my life: we visited, and then became enamored of, the Still River Monastery community at Still River, Massachusetts. The monastery, along with a nearby convent, was an isolated Catholic communal order of Brothers and Sisters, all of whom had taken pious vows of celibacy, poverty and religious pursuit, and were quite content to honor them. The Brothers had their responsibilities, the Sisters theirs, and except for meals, the Mass and vespers, their paths rarely crossed. The men spent most of their days tending the cattle (they sold the milk to a local dairy food distributor), repairing farming equipment and mending the facilities, while the women kept themselves busy in the kitchen and keeping the chapel in good condition. But whenever their paths did cross for services or meals, the Sisters had their own entrances, and the Brothers had theirs, and to use the improper entrance or exit was highly inappropriate—which I discovered once when I ran ahead of the other boys on the way to vespers and mistakenly decided to take a short cut.

The people at the monastery were genuinely hospitable and, as a family, we came to love them and the lifestyle they had chosen for themselves. Among all of the residents at Still River, it was Brother Dominic who really latched on to our family. And with the exception of Brother Peter, who was usually entertaining enough to keep all seven of the Kauffman children thoroughly entertained, it was Brother Dominic who captured our family's interest and affection the most. It was he who taught us true devotion to Mary, who taught us about the Rosary, and who taught us the most about being Catholic. Our affection for him would keep bringing us back to Still River even after we left Massachusetts when Dad retired three years later.

Upon retiring, Dad accepted a position at Linn-Benton Community College in Albany, Oregon. One of my sisters, the eldest of the seven children, went off to college at the University of California at Irvine before we left Worcester, and the remaining six moved with Mom and Dad to Albany. We quickly began to attend St. Mary's Catholic Church there, and again we rarely missed a service. For my part, I had just finished the sixth grade level at Our Lady of the Angels Elementary School in Worcester, so I enrolled in North Albany Junior High, a public school, while my two younger siblings attended St. Mary's Catholic school by the church.

The next year, Mom explained to me that sometimes young boys can spend summers at the Still River Monastery, just like summer camp, and if I cared to, the option was certainly available. I decided that I would rather enjoy it, and the summer between my eighth and ninth grade years I spent a whole month at the monastery. I talked with Brother Peter occasionally, but my mentor, teacher, friend, and catechist was Brother Dominic. That summer, he and I spent hours together clearing brush from the backwoods of the monastery property, mending old, rusted barbed wire fences, and tending the cattle in the dairy. Often we would rise at 5:30 in the morning and work with the cows until breakfast at 8:00, and then head out to the fields to work until lunch at noon. All the while, Brother Dominic tutored me in the ways of Catholicism. It was from him that I learned that there could be no salvation outside the Catholic Church, that Mary and the Apostles had been Catholic, and that the Hail Mary, with the exception of the Our Father, was the greatest prayer ever written.[*]

I was astonished to learn of the profoundly marvelous heritage I had received from my parents, a heritage which for years I had taken for granted. Brother Dominic told me stories about the popes, about the saints, about Mary and about the early

---

[*] It is only fair to point out that while some of these are documented and official doctrines of the Catholic Church, they are hardly accepted universally among Catholics. I only wish to indicate that it was under these circumstances that I came to appreciate the Church that had spawned me and to appreciate the role of Mary from a Catholic perspective. To my knowledge this monastery was later disbanded because of its unorthodox teachings. These beliefs would affect me for years to come regardless of whether all Catholics accept them or not.

Catholic martyrs. He told me that the number 72 was the perfect number because it was at the age of 72 that Mary was taken into Heaven and because there were 72 books in the Bible.* And above everything else, he taught me about Our Lady of the Rosary, the Brown Scapular of Our Lady of Mt. Carmel, Our Lady of the Miraculous Medal, and Our Lady of Fátima.

I was filled with awe, and before I left Still River at the end of that summer of 1979, Brother Dominic had given me a Rosary to pray with, and a Brown Scapular to wear along with a Miraculous Medal. But most importantly of all, he had given me a new faith and a new understanding of my Church. He had introduced me to the most compassionate, understanding, loving and powerful woman anyone could know: Mary.

Before leaving the monastery that summer, I purchased an extra Medal as a gift for my mother, and with my own Medal, Scapular and Rosary, I set off to practice my newfound faith. For reasons which I will soon explain, I felt quite sure of my salvation upon my departure from the monastery. My salvation intact, I left for Worcester to spend a few days with some friends of the family, instructing nearly every person I came across that I wished they would become Catholic so they would be able to go to Heaven. Then, before I left Worcester, I stopped by Blessed Sacrament Catholic Church to visit with Monsignor Haddad, a priest for whom I had frequently served as an altar boy, to let him know that one of the Kauffman children was considering the priesthood. He was pleased, to say the least, and instructed me to pray as if my life depended on it, promising that he would do the same. Then, having secured the blessings of the highest clergy I knew, I returned to Albany, Oregon in time to begin football practice that fall.

When it came time to pick numbers for our football uniforms I chose number 72 because of my new devotion to Mary. I

---

* This reflects the number of books in the Catholic Bible only. The number 72 comes from the 66 books which Protestants consider inspired plus the following seven books which are found in the Catholic Bible: Baruch, Judith, 1 and 2 Maccabees, Sirach, Tobit, Wisdom, chapters A,B,C,D,E and F of Esther and chapters 13 and 14 of Daniel. Some multiple books like 1 and 2 Maccabees are considered one book in some translations. I suspect that this is how Brother Dominic arrived at the number 72. I no longer consider the extra books and chapters inspired.

continued to wear the Miraculous Medal and the Brown Scapular during my ninth grade year, even during football games and practice. I remember especially clearly that both the Medal and the Scapular would creep up over my pads and out of my football jersey—so noticeably that the other boys on the team could see them. Occasionally, they would avail themselves of the opportunity to swing me around from the neck by using the leash that the metallic chain and brown cloth string provided. Humiliating? Yes. But my eternal security rested in those very necklaces, and I wasn't about to divest myself of the guarantee of salvation simply for the convenience of not being swung around by my neck during football practice.

You see, the Scapular and the Medal were not just reminders of my devotion to Mary—they were a guarantee that I would not have to spend much time in Purgatory upon my death as long as I died in the State of Grace—a privilege otherwise withheld from those who do not wear the religious Marian articles.

According to tradition, St. Simon Stock was visited by an apparition of Mary in the Year 1251 in Cambridge, England. During the visit the apparition gave him a garment to wear as a symbol of his devotion to her. It consisted of two pieces of cloth held together by strings and was worn over the shoulders so that the cloth pieces would rest simultaneously on the chest and the back of the wearer. The Scapular came with a guarantee which stated that "anyone who dies clothed in this shall not suffer eternal fire; and if wearing it they die, they shall be saved." It was in 1322 that Pope John XXII expanded on the guarantee by proclaiming the Sabbatine Privilege, whereby those who wore the Scapular faithfully and with consistent prayers to Mary, would be released from Purgatory on the first Saturday after their death.[9] This proclamation by John XXII was later considered apocryphal by many Catholic scholars,[10] but that was quite beyond my understanding and knowledge in ninth grade. Apocryphal or otherwise, I had been told of the privileges bestowed on the wearer of the Scapular, and I would not be denied them. Such

---

[9] Cruz, Joan Carroll, *Prayers and Heavenly Promises Compiled from Approved Sources*, (Rockford, IL: TAN Books and Publishers, ©1990) pp. 26-7

[10] Hardon, John A., S.J, *Modern Catholic Dictionary*, (Garden City, NY: Doubleday & Company, ©1980) pg. 476

controversy notwithstanding, the Sabbatine Privilege, defined by
Pope John XXII in 1322, was confirmed by 20 more popes after
him,[11] including Pope Paul V who in 1613 limited the benefits of
the scapular by defining that Mary, by her merits, aided souls in
Purgatory on Saturdays but did not necessarily release them.[12]

A similar privilege was guaranteed to the wearer of the
Miraculous Medal, the production and distribution of which was
mandated to St. Catherine Labouré by the apparition of Mary
which occurred to her at Rue de Bac, Paris, France in 1830.
Anyone faithful enough to wear the Medal consistently would
"receive great graces,"[13] and I wore it as consistently and as
faithfully as anyone could.

To my faithful trust in the Scapular and the Miraculous
Medal, I added the daily recitation of the Rosary—not just ten
Hail Marys, but fifty, and sometimes even one hundred fifty, if I
cared to go through all fifteen mysteries (five sorrowful, five
joyful and five glorious).[*] According to tradition, the Rosary was
given to St. Dominic Guzman in France by an apparition of Mary
in 1206, and along with the Rosary, the apparition also gave 15
specific promises which would accompany anyone who recited it
faithfully. The best of these was the eleventh promise: "Whatever
you shall ask through the Rosary, you shall obtain."[14] Completely
undaunted by what the secular world would have believed, I put
all my faith in the Rosary as instructed, and I did not have to wait
long to see that the promises were true.

Having just joined the football team upon my return from Still
River that summer, I was looking forward to a good season, and I
spent every Wednesday night before each game on my knees
reciting the Rosary, praying for the safety of the players and for a
victory for the team. As the season drew on I saw that the promise
was true, but in spite of our undefeated record, which I gladly
attributed to the Rosary, I was not being played by the coach at

---

[11] Walsh, William J., *Apparitions and Shrines of Heaven's Bright
Queen*, Volume 2, (New York: T. J. Carey, ©1904) pg. 176

[12] Hardon, pg. 476

[13] Ball, Ann, *A Litany of Mary*, (Huntington, IN: Our Sunday Visitor
Publishing Division, Our Sunday Visitor, Inc., ©1988) pg. 73

[*] Photographs of the Rosary, the Brown Scapular, and the Miraculous
Medal are shown on the back cover

[14] Ball, pp. 117-20

all. In fact, my recollection of that season is that I only played two minutes out of all the games combined. By the time our last game finally rolled around, undefeated as we were, I still had not been given the chance to prove myself. Out of frustration, I decided not to pray the Rosary for the team that Wednesday night, and sure enough, on Thursday when we played our last game, I saw the power of the Rosary displayed for the whole world to see: we tied. It was worse than a loss—to be that close to a perfect season just to have it denied the team at the last minute, even the last play. I was just as convinced as I ever had been, and the coach had gotten his just deserts for not playing me to the extent I had wished.

Does this sound selfish? Even foolish? It was. But to a ninth grader, to have wielded that much power was exhilarating, and the mediocrity that the last game now imposed on our season was enough to prove that the eleventh promise was right. I could have whatever I requested through the Rosary.

These events contributed to the development of my faith for another eight years, and I prayed the Rosary faithfully for a long time afterward, though I don't recall having worn the Scapular and Medal much beyond the tenth grade.* Regardless of this, I must say that my devotion to the Rosary and wearing the religious articles paled in comparison to my devotion to Our Lady of Fátima and the story of what she had done there. After all, was it not for her sake that I did the rest? It surely was. The Medal, the Scapular and the Rosary were just preliminary indications of Mary's devotion to the spiritual progress of her children, but the apparition at Fátima was the grand climax of her many demonstrations of faithfulness and love. As Brother Dominic had told me, Mary appeared at Fátima in 1917 to the children there, and after many visits, she had made the sun literally drop out of the sky to the ground in front of 70,000 eyewitnesses. The very idea of that happening made the football season seem insignificant, but I took both events to heart, and if I continued to pray the Rosary, it was to Our Lady of Fátima; if I wore my

---

* As an interesting side note, when I was in the 10th grade, my dog Fitzie was so seriously ill that I considered placing the Scapular on him, believing that he might recover because of it. For good or for bad, I was unable to locate the Brown Scapular, Fitzie did not recover, and now I don't care to know what would have happened had I found it.

Brown Scapular, it was for her protection that I did so; if I wore the Miraculous Medal, I did so to honor the Fátima apparition and receive many graces from Mary.

When my parents were divorced after three years in Oregon, Mom took the three youngest of us with her to Loveland, Colorado, and I carried the Fátima devotion with me there, too. We immediately began to attend the only Catholic Church in town and even donated a painting of an apparition of Mary to the church for a shrine that was being built there. Within a year of our arrival I received the Sacrament of Confirmation, and just like every other church we had attended until then, our participation was nothing short of admirable. I remember clearly once, when I was asked to read from 1 Corinthians during the Mass, I made a point of arriving early to spend some time on my knees in front of the Tabernacle where the consecrated bread and wine were kept. I found out later that this was called the Adoration of the Eucharist, which the apparition of Mary at Fátima had urged so strongly. Father Roger, the priest who offered the Mass that evening, told the whole congregation how impressed he was that I had arrived early to pray and that the clarity with which I had read from the passage that night was a testimony to my spiritual growth as a young man. I swelled up with pride, realizing that my outstanding devotion to Mary and to Jesus in the Eucharist had been paraded in front of the whole congregation.

I continued to attend Mass faithfully for years after that, and though I gradually let the Marian devotion slip away, I would always return to it in a time of crisis. I would remember Fátima and what Mary had done there and I would return to the daily recitation of the Rosary. Through college I prayed the Rosary when troubled times came, and when my first college roommate criticized Catholicism, I reminded him of Fátima and the love of Mary for the Church. When it came time to have my appendix removed, I was delighted to pray the Rosary in hopes of a full recovery, the prayers for which were answered.

It was during my sophomore year at college that I was beginning seriously to consider the Catholic priesthood again, and by the end of my junior year, I had visited both St. Thomas More Seminary in Denver and Conception Seminary College at St. Joseph, Missouri to see what the priesthood would be like. When I finally graduated from the University of Colorado, I confess I was no longer praying the Rosary faithfully. But when I moved to Alabama and people asked me about the apparitions of Mary occurring in various places, I would explain that Mary was just trying to reach people with the message of Jesus Christ. Certainly my enthusiasm had waned, but the foundation on which I had based my faith was laid thick with the Marian devotion that had so consumed me at an earlier age. It was on this foundation that I made my plans to move to Alabama, with every intention of proving conclusively that I was truly a Christian—something I was certain of but my Protestant friends doubted—and that the division between Protestants and Catholics needed to be seriously de-emphasized. After my arrival in Huntsville, I met some new friends and then began my search to find a Catholic Church in town and to become a strong, faithful Catholic for all the world to see. I intended to be sitting in a Catholic pew that first Sunday morning after my arrival.

I never made it there.

Contrapositive

What if we've fallen to the bottom of a well,
thinkin' we've risen to the top of a mountain?
What if we're knockin' at the gates of hell,
thinkin' we're Heaven bound?[15]
—Truth

TO be honest, I must make it clear that as a very young child I was hardly a theologically mature Catholic even though I was very diligent in pursuing the rituals that my faith had prescribed. As I have already said, I feigned sickness more than once to avoid Sunday church services, but I had also used this excuse to avoid the Stations of the Cross, Benediction, and other church-related events. I was in no way a zealous defender of the faith, nor did I care to be. In fact, even in the midst of my devotion to Mary in junior high school, I never even considered the notion of *understanding* my faith—much less actually *defending* it. Until high school. And when I decided that the time had come to defend my faith, I did so, not because of a religious experience through the Church proper or because of a sudden growth spurt in my spiritual life, but because my circumstances warranted such a defense.

I had met my first evangelical Protestant.

There would be more after him, and I was completely unprepared. It frustrated me greatly to be without answers as my Protestant friends quoted the Bible verse by verse, trying to tell

---

[15] From the song, "Living Life Upside Down," by Gary Driskell and Karla Worley from the album, *More Than You'll Ever Imagine*, by *Truth*. Copyright ©1991 by Word Music (a division of Word, Inc.) All rights reserved. Used by permission

me that it was the supreme authority, even over the pope. Not to be dissuaded by the arguments of the foolish, I soon began to dig into the Bible myself for the sole purpose of defending the doctrines I proclaimed but did not understand, and (this may come as a surprise to some Protestants) there are ways to defend the doctrines of the Catholic Church with Scripture, even those doctrines which are at the center of the division between Protestants and Catholics. And I learned them all. *Quid pro quo* — and verse for verse I was finally learning to defend the mother Church against the equally well-founded arguments of my non-Catholic friends — and quite well at that. Additionally, I was growing in maturity as a Catholic young man. I was building a sturdy structure on that thick foundation. It was, to say the least, very fulfilling to begin to understand the depths of the Church I had for so long professed as my own.

Why do I say this? To make the following point: the more I was confronted by people who threw verses around like so many bullets on some sort of spiritual battlefield, the more convinced I became that the mother Church was correct — after all, if the Reformation had fostered this much confusion about doctrines and methods of salvation, then certainly God would honor that Church which had contributed least to the division and bitterness that had followed. And besides, even if every doctrine of the Catholic Church could be proven wrong with some passage of Scripture, I was all the more convinced that those offering such arguments were so much the more evil for it. They were, after all, criticizing the very Church that Mary had decided to honor by her frequent visits — visits which were pathetically under-recognized by the worldwide Protestant populace. In short, with each confrontation I was driven further back into the Church with a newfound faith and a strengthened sense of even clannish or fraternal pride. And I would grow still more, often relishing the counterproductivity which resulted from the efforts of whomever had tried to redirect my path.

But since the time that I left the Catholic Church, I have often found myself in the opposite position — that of the aggressor — trying to convince a Catholic of his or her error, and always to my own frustration. Ultimately, I had to come to terms with the fact that my efforts were only serving to push the Catholic back to the Catholic Church without ever initiating any productive dialogue whatsoever.

So I believe I can honestly say that I have been on both sides of the fence. As a Catholic being accosted by Protestants, and as a Protestant confronting Catholics. I assure you, from all of my experience, I am convinced that it was never the message that failed, but the method. God promises that His Word will never go forth and return to Him without accomplishing the purpose for which He sent it,[*] and I am convinced that any of His words that I spoke were as appropriate as they could possibly be, but the method I had used was, and still is, regrettable. A method which never worked with me, I was so quick to try on others, as if there was to be no learning from other people's mistakes, or even from my own.

But now I would like to apply what I have learned, and to try something different, even if at first it might seem a little odd. I would like to initiate a discussion in this chapter—a discussion in which there is only one rule: all Catholic doctrines are assumed to be true. And we go from there.

I know this must sound silly considering my earlier statement that I intend to prove that the apparitions of Mary are not at all what they seem to be. However, I know how ineffective it can be to start a discussion in which the party with whom I wish to engage is immediately put on the defensive. Knowing this, I would like to exercise a bit of gentleman's license and put myself on the defensive, giving the home field advantage to the people whom I have quite possibly already offended beyond reparation. But, if my target audience is still reading, consider yourself to be in the strategically superior position since the burden of proof is now on me. You have nothing to lose since we agree from the beginning that your position is the correct one, and mine the errant. As I have said, this may seem odd and I hardly wish to make light of the discussion, but the consistent failure with my former methods certainly warrants a new, albeit unorthodox, approach.

Given these ground rules, we begin to narrow the breadth of the discussion down to those doctrines dealing specifically with Mary—that is, the doctrines of the Immaculate Conception of Mary and the Assumption of Mary into Heaven. We do so because, with one exception, doctrines other than these are quite beyond the scope of this book and had the reader wished to pursue them, he or she would certainly be reading a different

---

[*] Isaiah 55:11

book by now. I will assume that your continued reading implies consent to these limitations.

Since the definitions of these doctrines also find the basis of their authority in the Papal Bulls, or statements, from the popes who promulgated them, we must also bring into the discussion the doctrine of Papal Infallibility. After all, had Popes Pius IX and Pius XII not been speaking infallibly, then the doctrines they defined *ex cathedra* would hardly be worth considering. And remember, we are assuming these doctrines to be true, so we can start by saying that Mary was indeed conceived without sin, she was taken body and soul into Heaven at the termination of her earthly ministry, and the popes who defined such doctrines as worthy of Catholic faith were speaking *ex cathedra*, that is to say, "from the Chair" of St. Peter, and therefore inerrantly in the definition of an article of Christian faith.

For the sake of the non-Catholic reader, I will defer to the following doctrinal texts regarding the definitions of the applicable doctrines. They are as follows:

The Doctrine of the Immaculate Conception of Mary From the Papal Bull *Ineffabilis Deus* Issued by Pope Pius IX, 1854

"We, by the authority of our Lord Jesus Christ, of the blessed Apostles Peter and Paul, and by Our own authority declare, pronounce and define that the doctrine which holds that the Most Blessed Virgin Mary from the first moment of her conception was, by the singular grace and privilege of almighty God, in view of the merits of Christ Jesus the Saviour of the human race, preserved immune from all stain of original sin, is revealed by God and is therefore firmly and constantly to be believed by all the faithful."[16]

The Doctrine of the Assumption of Mary From the Apostolic Constitution *Munificentissimus Deus* Issued by Pope Pius XII, 1950

"Wherefore, having directed humble and repeated prayers to God, and having invoked the light of the Spirit of Truth, to the glory of Almighty God, who has bestowed

---

[16] Pope Pius IX, *Ineffabilis Deus*, December 8, 1854

His special bounty on the Virgin Mary, for the honour of his Son the immortal King of ages and Victor over sin and death, for the greater glory of his august Mother, and for the joy and exaltation of the whole Church, by the authority of our Lord Jesus Christ, of the blessed Apostles Peter and Paul, and by Our own, We proclaim and define it to be a dogma revealed by God that the immaculate Mother of God, Mary ever Virgin, when the course of her earthly life was finished, was taken up body and soul into the glory of heaven."[17]

The Doctrine of the Infallibility of the Pope From Vatican Council I, Session IV, 1870 Dogmatic Constitution *Pastor Aeternus*

"Therefore, faithfully adhering to the tradition received from the beginning of the Christian faith, for the glory of God our Saviour, the exaltation of the Catholic religion, and the salvation of Christian peoples, the Sacred Council approving, We teach and define that it is a dogma divinely revealed: that the Roman Pontiff, when he speaks *ex cathedra*, that is, when in discharge of the office of Pastor and Doctor of all Christians, by virtue of his supreme apostolic authority he defines a doctrine regarding faith and morals to be held by the Universal Church, by the divine assistance promised him in Blessed Peter, is possessed of that infallibility with which the Divine Redeemer willed that His Church should be endowed for defining doctrine regarding faith and morals: and that therefore such definitions of the Roman Pontiff are irreformable of themselves, and not from the consent of the Church."[18]

Now, assuming that these doctrines are true, we can begin our discussion, which I wish to do by assessing the development of the Assumption doctrine.

It was of great interest to me when I first started studying the doctrines to realize how intimately the first two were tied together. As it turns out, the doctrine of the Assumption found its basis in the doctrine of the Immaculate Conception, and justifiably so. For if Mary truly had been conceived without sin,

---

[17] Pope Pius XII, *Munificentissimus Deus*, AAS 42(1950):660
[18] Vatican Council I, Session IV, Chapter IV, July 18, 1870

then it was incomprehensible to believe that she should ever suffer the consequences of original sin—that is, bodily decay in the grave—from which, by the grace of God, she had been protected. The most noted Catholic theologians have found this to be the case, including G. Roschini, who spoke on this issue in a 1950 Vatican Radio address just prior to the declaration of the Assumption doctrine. He asserted that Mary's Immaculate Conception and her Assumption were so unbreakably interdependent "as to authorize us to say that she was assumed because she was immaculate."[19]

And true enough, the consequence of original sin, that is the sin which we inherit because of Adam and Eve, is death. God mentions this specifically as a consequence of rebellion before Adam and Eve had ever disobeyed. Genesis 2:16,17 reads,

> "And the LORD God commanded the man, saying, Of every tree of the garden thou mayest freely eat: But of the tree of the knowledge of good and evil, thou shalt not eat of it: for in the day that thou eatest thereof thou shalt surely die.'"

And then again, after they had disobeyed, God explained that His warning had come to pass:

> "In the sweat of thy face shalt thou eat bread, till thou return unto the ground; for out of it wast thou taken: for dust thou art, and unto dust shalt thou return."[20]

As is commonly known, this curse of 'dirt to dirt,' or 'dust to dust' literally means that we will all decay in the grave as a consequence of Adam's rebellion. As simple as this sounds, and as commonly as it is understood, I feel it necessary to return to this and establish that death is a consequence of sin, or as Paul said in Romans 6:23, "the wages of sin is death." It is precisely this "wage" to which Mary was made immune by virtue of her sinlessness. It is this curse, as Roschini explained, that could not possibly have been applied to Mary because if Mary were indeed subject to the curse, then how could she have been conceived without sin? Roschini was correct then when he suggested that the

---

[19] Roschini, G. M., "The Assumption and the Immaculate Conception," *The Thomist* 14 (1941) pg. 65 (As quoted in Duggan, pg. 6)
[20] Genesis 3:19

two doctrines are so interdependent that it must follow logically that Mary was assumed precisely *because* she was immaculate. This concept would be carried strongly into every pontificate from then on, even to that of John Paul II. In 1983, while on a pilgrimage to Lourdes, France, the sight of the 1858 apparitions, he "declared that the two mysteries of the Immaculate Conception and the Assumption of Mary into heaven come together here and 'reveal their mutual complementarity.'"[21]

So thoroughly intertwined are these two concepts that Pius XII saw fit to address and clarify the issues *infallibly* in his 1950 proclamation, *Munificentissimus Deus*, as he wrote,

> "Yet, according to the general rule, God does not will to grant to the just the full effect of the victory over death until the end of time has come. And so it is that the bodies of even the just are corrupted after death, and only on the last day will they be joined, each to its own glorious soul. Now God has willed that the Blessed Virgin Mary should be exempt from this general rule. She, by an entirely unique privilege, completely overcame sin by her Immaculate Conception, and as a result she was not subject to the law of remaining in the corruption of the grave, and she did not have to wait until the end of time for the redemption of her body."[22]

This preservation of Mary from any effect of sin was further supported by the notion long held dear to Catholics and virtually unknown to Protestants: that Mary, having been conceived without sin and therefore not subject to the curse of death, likewise could not have been subject to pain in childbirth, because that too had been a result of the fall of man—a consequence specifically reserved for women:

> "Unto the woman he said, I will greatly multiply thy sorrow and thy conception; in sorrow thou shalt bring forth children."[23]

---

[21] Pope John Paul II, "Marie, première figure de la Rédemption, Homélie à la mess du 15 aôut à Lourdes," *La Documentation Catholique* (4-18 September 1983): 827-828 (As quoted in Duggan, pg. 152)

[22] Pope Pius XII, *Munificentissimus Deus*, AAS 42(1950):770

[23] Genesis 3:16a

Since this curse was assigned to Eve and to all women as a result of the fall, and since Mary, by virtue of her Immaculate Conception and by the grace of God was born outside of the bloodline of Adam, she was also granted immunity from the 'pangs of childbearing.' Establishing this fact was especially important to the doctrine of Mary's Perpetual Virginity, for while it was understood Biblically that Mary's *physical* virginity was preserved during Christ's conception, it was equally important that her *physical* virginity be preserved during childbirth. Pope Leo the Great made this clear when he wrote,

> "He was conceived of the Holy Spirit in the womb of His Virgin Mother who brought Him forth without detriment to her virginity, as, too, she had, without detriment to her virginity, conceived Him."[24]

Since her flesh was preserved in childbirth, her childbirth must have caused her no pain. She was, after all, not subject to sin's consequences. And if Mary's Immaculate Conception was to be the basis on which the assertion of pain-free childbirth was built, then Mary's freedom from pain in delivering Christ was an equally solid foundation on which the doctrine of the Assumption could be constructed. This has long since been confirmed by Pope Alexander III who in the 12th century stated explicitly that Mary had given birth to Christ without pain:

> "Mary conceived without detriment to her virginity, gave birth to her Son without pain, and departed hence without being subject to corruption."[25]

As the doctrine matured, a new issue was naturally raised as theologians began to wonder if Mary had even died at all since corruption *and* death were both the result of the fall in which Mary had played no part. For that matter, disease was a result of the fall as well, so the issue of Mary's death was carried so far as to suggest that even if Mary had died, her death certainly had not

---

[24] From the *Tome* of Pope St. Leo the Great, a letter to Flavian, the bishop of Constantinople, June 13, 449

[25] *Virgin Wholly Marvelous: Praises of Our Lady from the Popes, Councils, Saints, and Doctors of the Church*, Peter Brookby, ed., (Cambridge, England: The Ravengate Press, ©1981) pg. 96

been caused by disease,[26] because she had been shielded from the original sin which had caused disease in the first place.

This issue was by no means left unconsidered in the final definition of the dogma of the Assumption of Mary. During the deliberations prior to the proclamation, various petitions were submitted regarding the issue of Mary's death. While there was substantial disagreement about the end of Mary's life, there was a general reluctance to discuss the issue of her death since it might betray her presumed sinlessness, on which the Assumption doctrine was to be based:

> "Out of the 3,019 petitions of what may be termed the teachers in the Church, 2,344 do not mention the issue, 5 seem to doubt our Lady's death, 24 seem to affirm her death but do not do so clearly, 434 (including 264 residential bishops) affirmed that our Lady died, [but] do not wish her death defined but rather placed in preambulatory argument or exposition; finally, 212 (including 154 residential bishops) wish her death included in the definition itself of the Assumption."[27]

All petitions aside, though, you will recall that the final wording of the doctrine stated that Mary had been assumed 'when the course of her earthly life was finished.' Thereby, those who wished to interpret that to mean 'when she died' could do so, and those who wished to understand it as 'when her ministry was complete, but before death' could do so as well. It was specific enough in describing the Assumption, yet vague enough to allow for the interpretation of many methods of assumption, whether they be *post mortem* or otherwise. The point being that even those who argued for the wording to include Mary's death (after all, even Jesus died) still believed in the Assumption for the very simple reason that Mary's sinless body could hardly undergo corruption (i.e., decomposition) because Jesus' sinless body certainly had not. So in spite of the many different understandings

---

[26] Duggan, Paul E., *The Assumption Dogma: Some Reactions and Ecumenical Implications in the Thought of English-Speaking Theologians*, (Dayton, OH: International Marian Research Institute, ©1989) pg. 61

[27] Carter, "The Assumption," pp. 425-32, (As quoted in Duggan, pg. 43). Brackets added for clarity, parentheses in original

of the circumstances of the Assumption, the year 1950 ended with a unanimously approved and divinely revealed doctrine regarding Mary's immediate bodily transport into Heaven when she departed from earth.

*   *   *

Now to this point I have not yet addressed the key issue of this book—that is, the apparitions—but it was important that we first establish, based on the teachings of the Catholic Church, that Mary was conceived without sin and was therefore not subject to its consequences. She conceived Christ without detriment to her physical virginity, gave birth to Him without pain, and left the earth without corruption to her body. There was no sin, and therefore no bodily corruption at any time in her life. In fact, regarding the matter of sin, St. Augustine would not allow the topic to be discussed if the purpose was to question Mary's exemption from it:

> "With the exception therefore of the Holy Virgin Mary, with regard to whom, when sin is in question, I cannot, out of respect of Our Lord, permit any discussion."[28]

And I, too, would happily let the matter rest there were it not for the fact that the followers of the apparitions of Mary have unwittingly introduced the topic of sin into this discussion. Therefore, I simply cannot avoid what has to be introduced next.

When the apparition of Mary makes its many appearances, it usually does so with a crown of twelve stars around its head. This has been the case at the Rue de Bac, Paris apparitions in 1830 and at Medjugorje, Bosnia from 1981 to the present. During the Rue de Bac apparitions, known also as the apparitions of Our Lady of the Miraculous Medal, Mary was said to have appeared with a crown of twelve stars and standing on the moon. The statue of Our Lady of the Miraculous Medal at Rue de Bac, Paris portrays the apparition in such a manner. The visions are referred to by the name of the Miraculous Medal because the apparition requested that Catherine Labouré, the Rue de Bac visionary, stamp and

---

[28] St. Augustine, *De Natura et Gratia*, 36, 42

distribute a medal in honor of the visits. Catherine describes the encounter:

> "At this moment, where I was or was not I do not know, an oval shape formed around the Blessed Virgin, and on it were written these words in letters of gold: 'O Mary conceived without sin, pray for us who have recourse to thee.'
>
> "Then a voice was heard to say: 'Have a medal struck after this model. Those who wear it will receive great graces; abundant graces will be given to those who have confidence.' ...Suddenly, the oval seemed to turn. I saw the reverse of the medal: the letter M surmounted by a cross, and below it two hearts, one crowned with a crown of thorns, and the other pierced by a sword. I seemed to hear a voice which said to me: 'The M and the two hearts say enough.'"[29]

The two hearts which appeared below the letter 'M' are the Sacred Heart of Jesus and the Immaculate Heart of Mary, but of special importance is what surrounds the image stamped on the back side of the 'Miraculous Medal.' On the front is an image of Mary standing on the moon with a serpent under her feet and a halo about her head, with the words, 'O Mary, conceived without sin, pray for us who have recourse to thee,' inscribed around her image, just as Catherine Labouré described. But on the reverse, around the two hearts aflame, are twelve stars symmetrically placed about the perimeter of the medal.[30]

Those who circulate pamphlets, tracts and other information about the various apparitions are certainly outspoken on this particular issue of the twelve stars. In a pamphlet describing the Medjugorje events during which Jakov Colo received an apparition, they write:

> "This is Medjugorje. In Medjugorje Our Lady wants to save the whole world. Our Lady is coming as a mother whose children are in a house which is on fire. How does the Miraculous Medal fit in? There are twelve stars around the medal. These twelve stars have been

[29] Ball, pg. 73

[30] Aradi, Zsolt, *Shrines to Our Lady Around the World*, (New York: Farrar, Straus and Young, ©1954) pp. 94-5

> seen by the visionaries in Medjugorje to this day at
> every apparition. In the beginning, little Jakov said,
> 'She has twelve stars around her head. The stars are
> just as in Church except Hers don't have wires holding
> them up.' The significance of the stars is Biblical and,
> in themselves, a great sign."[31]

The pamphlet continues by referring to Revelation 12:1, and then goes on to describe the significance of the sun and the moon in the prophecy:

> "In Medjugorje Our Lady appears on the mountain
> to one or two of the visionaries most Monday nights.
> Many times on Her returning to Heaven, they describe
> Our Lady as leaving in the light of the sun. One could
> describe it as Revelation does, 'clothed with the sun.'
> "Saint Catherine said the globe she saw in Our
> Lady's hands represented the earth. The globe Her feet
> rested on was described only as a globe of which only
> one half could be seen. Is this the moon about Her feet
> which Revelation describes? It is hard to deny. Even in
> France, the Statue that depicts what St. Catherine saw
> looks like the moon underneath Our Lady's feet."[32]

But does Revelation 12:1 really refer to Mary? Countless thousands believe that it does and their numbers include some very notable Catholic leaders. Pope Pius XII, proclaimer of the Assumption doctrine, made reference to the twelve stars in the Assumption Prayer which he composed especially for the ceremony during which the new dogma would be proclaimed:

> "We believe finally that in the glory where you reign,
> clothed with the sun and crowned with stars, you are,
> after Jesus, the joy and gladness of all the angels and
> the saints."[33]

---

[31] *Medjugorje: The Fulfillment of All Marian Apparitions?*,
(Birmingham, AL: Saint James Publishing Company, ©1991) pg. 13.
The pamphlet's author wished to remain anonymous and is listed only
as, "A friend of Medjugorje."

[32] *Medjugorje: The Fulfillment of All Marian Apparitions?*, pp. 13-4

[33] Doheny, William J., C.S.C., J.U.D., and Kelly, Joseph P., S.T.D.,
Papal Documents on Mary, (Milwaukee: The Bruce Publishing
Company, ©1954) pg. 241

Then, in 1983, while Pope John Paul II was in France, he visited Lourdes, "not only to honor the Virgin in her heavenly birth but also in her earthly conception and birth."[34] Of Mary, John Paul II said,

> "...Behold! Here is what was spoken about in the book of [Revelation]: 'The Dragon stopped in front of the woman as she was having the child, so that he could eat it as soon as he was born from its mother.'"[35]

Given this consistent papal reference to the woman of Revelation 12, the mantle of the sun and the crown of stars, it is not surprising at all that the apparitions, in addition to appearing with a crown of twelve stars, actually confirm that the understanding of the popes is correct. The apparition at Agreda, Spain in the early 1600s explained the meaning of the verse in question and confirmed to the visionary there that the Woman of Revelation 12 is Mary:

> "The crown of twelve stars are evidently all the virtues, with which that Queen of heaven and earth was to be adorned. But the mystery of its being composed of twelve stars has reference to the twelve tribes of Israel, by which all the elect and the predestined are designated, as is mentioned in the seventh chapter of [Revelation] by [St. John] the Evangelist. And since the gifts, graces and virtues of all the elect were to crown their Queen in a most eminent and exalted degree, a crown of twelve stars was placed around her head."[36]

And in 1989 at San Nicolás, Argentina, the apparition supported this interpretation:

---

[34] Duggan, pp. 153-4

[35] Pope John Paul II, "Marie, première figure de la Rédemption, Homélie à la mess du 15 aôut à Lourdes," *La Documentation Catholique* (4-18 September 1983): 827-828. Brackets added for clarity. The book of Revelation is referred to as "the Apocalypse" in the original. (As quoted in Duggan, pg. 154)

[36] Mary of Agreda, *Mystical City of God: The Divine History and Life of the Virgin Mother of God*, Volume I, *The Conception*, (Hammond, IN: W. B. Conkey Company, ©1914) pg. 98, para. 99. Brackets added

> "The Lord has marked this time with a sign; the
> Woman clothed with the sun ([Revelation] 12:1). She
> represents the hope to which her children must
> cling."[37]

Without doubt, the papacy has proclaimed it, the apparition
has confirmed it and many of the lay people had believed it all
along anyway. Mary is not only the Woman of Revelation 12, but
the apparitions are the fulfillment of that specific prophecy.[*] And
for its part, the apparition has done nothing to indicate anything to
the contrary. As can be seen in the many shrines to Mary around
the world (see Table 1 on page 47), the portrayal of the Madonna
with a full or crescent moon about her feet and/or a crown of stars
(usually 12) around her head is almost universal.

Now, after nearly 15 pages of apologetics about these
doctrines, I suppose that the reader is saying, "Yes, but *why* are
you telling me?" Well, I have arrived at the point where I must
tell you why, but there is a good reason for the depth to which I
have researched these doctrines and there is a good reason that I
have described their origins in such detail.

We have assumed them to be true, we have assumed the Papal
Bulls to be infallible and we have assumed that the Church's
position on approved apparitions is true as well. So if it is all true,
what's the point?

Remember, if you will, the discussion that went into the
refining of the Assumption doctrine. What were the issues? Could
the Immaculate Mary have *died* if death is a consequence of sin?
Could Immaculate Mary's body experience *decomposition* if
bodily corruption is a consequence of sin? Could the Immaculate
Mary experience *disease*, if disease was caused by the rebellion of
man? Could Immaculate Mary have experienced the *pangs of*

---

[37] *Our Lady Queen of Peace*, "An Urgent Appeal: Our Lady in
Argentina," pg. 7. Brackets added for clarity. The book of Revelation is
referred to as "the Apocalypse" in the original. Message of February 28,
1989. Used by permission

[*] Since only a handful of apparitions have been approved as worthy of
devotion by the Church, I would be remiss to suggest that the Church
believes that *all* apparitions are the fulfillment of the Revelation 12
prophecy. It would be more accurate to say that the Church believes that
approved apparitions are the fulfillment of the Revelation 12 prophecy.

childbirth if painful childbirth is a consequence of the fall of man? Did Immaculate Mary ever, *ever* experience anything at all that was a result of sin? How could she? She was conceived completely, absolutely and totally without sin and therefore not subject to its consequences. That much we have determined to be true in the discussion. All assumptions have proved to be true based on the absolute truth contained in Catholic doctrines.

So what does Revelation 12:1 really say? I ask you to read the following verses very carefully. They are quoted from Revelation 12:1,2 of the New American Bible, an approved translation of the Catholic Church:

> "A great sign appeared in the sky, a woman clothed with the sun, with the moon under her feet, and on her head a crown of twelve stars. She was with child and wailed aloud in pain as she labored to give birth."

Look at the words closely. *"Wailed aloud in pain as she labored to give birth."* Remember that the pangs of childbirth are a result of the fall of man. The consequence of sin. If mankind had never fallen, women would experience virtually painless childbirth. *Any* woman not under the curse would experience pain-free childbearing. But the Woman of Revelation 12:1,2 is clearly experiencing a consequence of sin.

A problem is now introduced and the ground rules we agreed to follow at the beginning of this chapter no longer serve to clarify the issue. For example, "it was always taught in the Church that sin can never be associated with Mary."[38] However, we are now given two mutually exclusive options: 1) Scripture is correct and the Woman of Revelation 12 is experiencing the pangs of childbirth, a consequence of sin, and therefore cannot be Mary, or 2) the apparition is correct in identifying itself both as the Woman of Revelation 12 and as Mary, and therefore is contradicting the Church's position on Mary's sinlessness. We cannot accept both options, and the latter must be removed from consideration since it defies the assumptions with which we initiated this discussion.

You must understand the significance of this problem, because if it is carried to its completion, it stands to undermine the

---

[38] Duggan, pg. 19

Shrine	Location	# of Stars	Standing on Moon
Our Lady of Grace	Milan, Italy	8	unknown
Our Lady of Czestochowa	Czestochowa, Poland	9	no
Blessed Virgin Mary of the Philippines	Santa Rosa, Philippines	12	unknown
Our Lady of Guadalupe	Guadalupe, Mexico	12	no
Our Lady of Mt. Carmel	Mt. Carmel, Italy	12	unknown
Our Lady of Ollignies	Ollignies, Belgium	12	unknown
Our Lady of Pompeii	Pompeii, Italy	12	crescent
Our Lady of Sorrows	Grenada, Spain	12	unknown
Our Lady of the Atonement (painting)	Garrison, New York, USA	12	full moon
Our Lady of the Cape	Cap de la Madeleine, Canada	12	unknown
Our Lady of the Miraculous Medal	Rue de Bac, Paris	12	full moon
Our Lady of Vocations	Slingerlands, New York, USA	12	no
The Miraculous Statue	Csiksomlyo-Sumuleu, Romania	12	crescent
The Virgin of Copacabana	Copacabana, Bolivia	12	crescent
Virgen del Pilar	Saragossa, Spain	12	unknown
Nuestra Señora de la Macarena	Seville, Spain	18	unknown
Our Lady of Covadonga	Covadonga, Spain	21	none
Our Lady of the Rosary of the Philippines	Manila, Philippines	25	none
Our Lady of San Juan de los Lagos	San Juan, Mexico	none	crescent
Our Lady of Lujan	Cordova, Argentina	none	crescent

Table 1: Shrines to Mary Around the World[39]

---

[39] Information contained in Table 1 comes from *Shrines to Our Lady Around the World*, and *A Litany of Mary*, both of which are referred to in the bibliography.

very foundations of the Catholic Church. For if the Woman described in Revelation 12:1,2 is actually Mary, which the apparition would have us believe, then Mary was suffering labor pains in childbirth — a veritable detriment to her physical virginity and certainly a consequence of sin. But the Church has already said this is impossible. That is, 'sin can never be associated with Mary,' which is why her painless childbirth was used as a basis for the Assumption dogma.

If the Woman of Revelation 12 is Mary, that would mean that Mary was not sinless, and therefore not conceived immaculately, meaning that the Papal Bull *Ineffabilis Deus* was not infallible. Which would mean Mary would not have been preserved from corruption or from decay in the grave because she would not have merited exclusion from it by her sinlessness. Which would mean that the argument for her Assumption falls apart, and with it, the Apostolic Constitution *Munificentissimus Deus* which defined it. We can say this because "when defining the Immaculate Conception, Pius IX doctrinally asserted that Mary had been preserved from sin and corruption; thus the Immaculate Conception and the Assumption shared the same foundation."[40] And as Roschini has said, we are authorized 'to say that she was assumed *because* she was immaculate.' In his words, these two doctrines are bound together by an 'unbreakable link,' because if Mary was Immaculate, she *had* to be Assumed.

But if Mary experienced birth pains as described in Revelation 12:2, then she was obviously not immaculate.

And if she was *not* immaculate, then she was *not* assumed, because the doctrine of her Assumption was based *entirely* on the merits of her Immaculate Conception. If she was *not* immaculate, then she was *not* assumed, because there would be nothing about her that merited exclusion from labor pains, much less the more serious consequences of sin: disease, death and corruption in the grave.

And if she was not assumed, then the Assumption doctrine was errant, and likewise, the doctrine of Infallibility on which the Assumption and the Immaculate Conception dogmas rest.

But, as Duggan wrote in *The Assumption Dogma*, "If the Assumption were false, then God would be responsible for

---

[40] Duggan, pg. 3

preserving his Church in error: an intrinsic impossibility,"[41] because, "the Holy Spirit resides permanently in the Church, ...[and therefore] her every judgment is attributable to the Spirit, the custodian of truth: 'An error of such proportion on such a subject would be the triumph of error in the teaching Church, which is of course an impossibility.'"[42] Thus, associating Mary with the Woman of Revelation 12 creates a myriad of doctrinal problems which are not easily resolved.

Perhaps the followers of the apparition of Mary recognize this problem, too. *Caritas of Birmingham*, in its promotional cassette tape about the apparitions of Mary in Medjugorje, carefully omits the second half of verse 2 when this part of Revelation 12 is read. In the audio tape entitled, "Between Heaven & Earth," the narrator begins by stating the following:

> "And a great sign appeared in heaven, a woman clothed with the sun, with the moon under her feet and on her head a crown of twelve stars. And she was with child."[43]

It is the remainder of verse 2 that causes the problems, so it was left unquoted in the promotional tape. Even the footnotes to the 1986 Revised New Testament of the New American Bible, a Catholic translation, acknowledge the source of the woman's pain, for it is clarified with the following statement: "Because of Eve's sin, the woman gives birth in distress and pain." The followers of the apparition of Mary, though, insist that the Woman of Revelation 12 is Mary, and seem to have a vested interest in making sure that the second half of Revelation 12:2 is not properly applied.

But one person in particular has taken this to an extreme: the apparition of Mary, itself. And when the apparition of Mary explained this puzzling verse to Sister Mary of Agreda in Spain, it did so by suggesting that St. John, the author of Revelation, really meant 'sorrow' where the word 'pain' appears in the verse:

---

[41] Duggan, pg. 17

[42] Carter, pg. 432 (As quoted in Duggan, pg. 16). Brackets added for clarity

[43] "Between Heaven & Earth," an audio tape of the Medjugorje story, produced and directed by Caritas of Birmingham TLM Ministries, tape #4404, ©1991, all rights reserved. Used by permission

> "He does not say this because She was to give birth in
> bodily pain, for that is not possible in this divine
> Parturition.* But because it was to be a great sorrow
> for that Mother to see that divine Infant come forth
> from the secrecy of her virginal womb in order to
> suffer and die as a victim for the satisfaction of the
> sins of the world. ...The Most High had determined to
> exempt Her from guilt, but not from the labors and
> sorrows corresponding to the reward, which was
> prepared for Her. Thus the sorrows of this birth were
> not the effect of sin, as they are in the descendants of
> Eve, but they were the effect of the intense and perfect
> love of the most holy Mother for her divine Son."[44]

This would probably be an acceptable interpretation of the
verse were it not for the fact that the apparition, in its exposition
of Revelation 12:2, contradicts the infallible teaching of the pope
who defined the Assumption dogma in the first place. The clear
teaching of Pope Pius XII was that Mary *did not* experience
sorrow when she was giving birth to Jesus. In the text of his *ex
cathedra* decree *Munificentissimus Deus*, Pius XII quotes John
Damascene, an eighth century theologian who is considered "the
great doctor of the Assumption."[45] Damascene wrote, and
Pius XII infallibly confirmed, that the sword of sorrow which
Simeon said would pierce Mary's heart did not do so until long
after Christ's birth—that is, at the cross—and that Mary had been
completely free of that painful sorrow when she gave birth to
Him:

> "It was fitting that she who had seen her Son upon the
> Cross and who had thereby received into her heart the
> sword of sorrow *which she had escaped in the act of
> giving birth to Him* should look upon Him as He sits
> with the Father."[46]

---

* Parturition: the action or process of giving birth to offspring.
(Webster's New Collegiate Dictionary)

[44] Mary of Agreda, *Mystical City of God*, Volume I, *The Conception*,
pp. 99-100, para. 102

[45] Duggan, pg. 27

[46] Pope Pius XII, *Munificentissimus Deus*, AAS 42(1950):761.
Emphasis added. Pius XII quotes from John Damascene, "Encomium in
Dormit.," Hom. 2, 14, pg. 96, 741B

In fact, the Scriptures testify that Mary had not even been informed of the sword of sorrow until eight full days after Christ was born. At the time of Jesus' circumcision Mary's sorrow was known to be a still future event.* In spite of this, the apparition attributes the labor pains to the sword of sorrow that would pierce Mary's heart—that is, God had decided 'to exempt Her from guilt, but not from the labors and sorrows corresponding to the reward.' But God inspired Pius XII to proclaim precisely the opposite in the divinely revealed dogma contained in the Apostolic Constitution *Munificentissimus Deus* when he stated that Mary had not experienced any sorrow in childbirth at all.

Therefore, in order to assume the identity of the Woman of Revelation 12, the apparition of Mary must first necessarily contradict the teaching of the papacy on Mary's sinlessness, and then must also contradict the teachings of Scripture on Mary's sword of sorrow and the meaning of birth pangs as a consequence of sin. But such contradictions are unacceptable. Those who propagate the messages of the apparition agree, for they state unequivocally that the words of Mary are not on the same level as the Bible:

> "So it is in this context that the messages of Medjugorje have to be understood. They are below the Bible, the inspired Word of God, but above all the books containing the greatest human wisdom and thought in all the world, throughout the ages... Are they on an equal with the Bible? Definitely NO!"[47]

I agree. We must accept the testimony of the Word over that of the apparition, and when the Bible gives the reason for the woman travailing in such pain, it simply states that the pain occurred because 'she was with child.' It does not say 'because the child would have so much to suffer,' nor that the pains 'were the effect of the intense and perfect love of the most holy Mother for her divine Son' as the apparition asserts. The Bible merely

---

* Luke 2:35

[47] *Understanding Our Lady's Messages*, (Birmingham, AL: Saint James Publishing Company, ©1991) pp. 13,11. The pamphlet's author wished to remain anonymous and is listed only as, "A friend of Medjugorje." Emphasis in original

states that the woman is in terrific pain because she was with child. Nothing more. And this is a consequence of sin, in which case the apparition's exposition of Revelation 12 is now in question since it contradicts the testimony of the Word.

This issue could go far beyond that of the apparitions of Mary, for while it is clear that the apparitions by identifying themselves as the Woman of Revelation 12 have contradicted the teachings of the papacy on Mary's painless childbirth, what can be said of the popes who alternately claim that Mary is the Woman of Revelation 12 and then that Mary experienced no pain in childbirth? That contradiction is equally disturbing, but it certainly must remain a separate topic. For now, the meaning of Revelation 12 must be interpreted in light of Catholic truth: birth pangs are the result of the fall of man; the Woman of Revelation 12 is experiencing them; Mary cannot experience them; therefore the Woman of Revelation 12 cannot be Mary.

It is with this understanding that we begin to realize that if the passage in Revelation is truly to be fulfilled by a woman appearing in the sky with twelve stars around her head, clothed with the sun and with the moon about her feet, then it cannot possibly be Mary who fulfills it. This is because the woman who fulfills the prophecy must be a woman who is tainted with sin— else, how could she be travailing in the pangs of childbirth? She must be a woman who was not conceived immaculately, which means the apparition is clearly in error on this point. And if its teachings are now in question, then the apparition's identity must be called into question as well. The apparition of Mary cannot possibly be who it claims to be.

We arrived at this point by assuming all Catholic doctrines to be true, and we cannot accept a conclusion which leads us to deny the assumptions we made in order to arrive there. And since the doctrines of the Church cannot be wrong, we must therefore believe that the apparition *is*. That is to say, we must either believe that the Church is wrong in defining the doctrines, and that God is therefore 'responsible for preserving his Church in error,' or that the apparition is wrong in claiming to be both Mary and the Woman of Revelation 12. But the Church cannot err, so the latter is the only conclusion we can make: the apparition of Mary is not at all who it claims to be.

Fortunately, even though the Assumption dogma is a matter of obligatory faith according to the *ex cathedra* proclamation by

Pius XII,[48] belief in the apparitions is not, according to a proclamation by Pope Benedict XIV in the 18th century.[49] Therefore, even though Catholics are required to believe in the Assumption as a matter of faith, they are not required to believe in the apparitions of Mary, *and are free to reject them.* An inspection of the apparitions demands that we do.

Thus, the conclusion we come to about the apparitions happens to be the only conclusion that can be properly reconciled with the doctrines of the Church, and is the only conclusion a Catholic can come to and truly remain Catholic. Indeed, both the Immaculate Conception and the Assumption doctrines are accompanied by a stern warning that if anyone should dare to "think otherwise" or "dare to deny what We have defined," they have "fallen from the unity of the Church" and have "abandoned the divine and Catholic faith."[50] There simply is no room for accepting the apparitions in light of the fact that they call these two doctrines into question.

Which means that the woman appearing to the children of Medjugorje, who appeared to the visionaries of Fátima, Lourdes, Paris and elsewhere around the world with twelve stars for her crown as if she was the Woman of Revelation 12; as if she was Immaculate Mary; as if she was the Mother of Jesus, temporarily excusing herself from Heaven to bring us a very important message, cannot possibly be the Mary to whom these doctrines of the Catholic Church have been ascribed.

Which means that the thing that is appearing as Mary in countless locations around the world, and has been for some eight hundred years, has been masquerading all this time as *someone it could not possibly be.*

Which means that whoever or whatever it is has been lying to us.

On purpose.

---

[48] Duggan, pg. 42

[49] Zimdars-Swartz, Sandra L., *Encountering Mary*, (New York: Princeton University Press, ©1991) pg. 9. The distinction here is the difference between *fides catholica* and *fides humana*, or Catholic vs. human faith. The difference is what requires Catholics to believe in the Assumption, while making devotion to the apparitions optional.

[50] From Papal Bull *Ineffabilis Deus* (Pius IX) and *Munificentissimus Deus*, AAS 42(1950):770 (Pius XII)

Modus Operandi

> 'Do you see what I see? ...Do you hear what I
> hear?' said the shepherd boy to the mighty king.
> —*popular Christmas carol*

BEFORE we begin to discuss the apparitions themselves and the messages they deliver I think it appropriate to discuss the methods the apparitions use. While at first they may seem strange, I ask the skeptic to withhold judgment until the discussion is complete because, as it turns out, the methods of interaction all have precedent incidents in the Bible. These will be discussed momentarily.

There is a certain vocabulary with which the apparitions and their messages must be understood. For example, if I use the terms 'inner locution' or 'intellectual vision,' it might be difficult to understand exactly what it is I am trying to say. Or if I tell you that the children at Medjugorje, Bosnia sometimes experience 'imaginative visions' while the children at Garabandal, Spain tended to experience 'inner locutions,' it still doesn't help you to understand precisely what the children experienced.

So, before I discuss exactly what it is that the children feel and see when they encounter an apparition of Mary, or what it is that the apparition is telling them, I saw fit to include a few definitions:

> **Apparition**: An actual visual, audible, physical encounter with a supernatural being. An apparition is not a hallucination and neither is it a figment of a visionary's imagination. Normally, the 'person' appearing is only visible to the

visionary, but occasionally, apparitions have been seen by many thousands of people at once.[51]

Ecstasy: This is the state in which a visionary receives an apparition, so named because of the appearance of extreme pleasure on the face of the recipient during the encounter. Ecstasy is a psychological term used to describe such a trance.

Exterior locution: "This is like an inner locution (see *Inner locution* and *Interior locution*, below) except that the person hears an audible voice through the ear."[52]

Imaginative vision: "This term does not mean that the vision is a figment of the visionary's own imagination but that God somehow manages to suspend reality and, using images that make sense to that person, infuses wisdom into the soul. This type of vision is more like a 'wide awake dream' while the real world has disappeared."[53]

Inner locution: "This is a supernatural means of communication. It is not a sensory communication since none of the five bodily senses are involved. They are messages given in very clear words which are not formed in the mind of the person, but in the heart while the mind of the person is at rest."[54]

Intellectual vision: This would be more accurately described as the feeling of having a newfound purpose after a supernatural encounter. It has more to do with advancing a goal than actually seeing anything.[55]

---

[51] For example, in Zeitun, Egypt from 1968-1970, and Betania, Venezuela on March 24th, 1984. Both of these sites included public apparitions to many people at once. See "Betania: Land of Grace," a video narrated by Ricardo Montalban. Directed, written and produced by Drew J. Mariani, Marian Communications, Ltd., ©1993

[52] *To Bear Witness that I Am the Living Son of God, Vol. 1: Reported Teachings and Messages to the World from Our Lord and Our Loving Mother*, (Newington, VA: Our Loving Mother's Children, ©1991) pg. iii

[53] *To Bear Witness*, pg. ii

[54] *To Bear Witness*, pp. ii-iii

[55] *To Bear Witness*, pp. ii

Interior locution: Same as an *Inner locution*.

Outer locution: Same as *Exterior locution*.

It is important to understand that it is by one of these five methods, accompanied by various degrees of ecstasy, that a visionary receives an apparition or a locution. Sometimes a message may come by inner locution without being accompanied by an apparition, and sometimes a message may be delivered in person by an apparition of Mary during which the visionary will be able to converse with and actually touch the figure. On some occasions, the apparition will appear alternately as Jesus and Mary, and sometimes even as Jesus, Mary, and St. Michael the Archangel together, or some other permutation of those three. The apparitions around the world are by no means consistent with respect to whom it is that actually appears, with what frequency, or with which method of interaction. One thing that is consistent, though, is that onlookers will see only the silent, moving lips and the ecstatic look on the face of the visionaries to indicate that an apparition is actually taking place.

I know there are skeptics who will not believe that the apparitions are occurring because the methods seem out of the ordinary, but again, I remind you that strangeness of method is not an indicator by which we may measure adherence to doctrinal truth. Just read Ezekiel 4 and Hosea 1 and you will see God using very strange methods indeed. There are many cases recorded in both the Old and New Testaments in which God used one or a combination of the above-described methods to communicate something to the Hebrews or to the believers in the newly founded Christian Church (see Table 2 on page 57). This being the case, we can safely say that various degrees of oddity and unorthodoxy are not valid criteria by which the authenticity of the apparitions can be justifiably dismissed. But again, I point this out not to convince anyone that the apparitions are from God; I only wish (at this point) to demonstrate that they are *real*, so please don't walk away from this now and feel that I have provided evidence that the apparitions are really from God. They are not. But they *do* use reasonable methods which, when compared against certain New Testament passages, might convince someone that they were.

Description of Event	Scripture Reference	Type of experience
Angel tells Joseph to take Mary as his wife	Matthew 1:20,21	Imaginative vision, Inner locution
Angel tells Joseph to flee to Egypt	Matthew 2:13	Imaginative vision, Inner locution
Angel instructs Joseph to return to Israel	Matthew 2:19	Imaginative vision, Inner locution
Jesus' baptism	Matt. 3:13-17, Mark 1:9-11, Luke 3: 21,22, John 1:29-34	Apparition, Intellectual vision
The Transfiguration	Matthew 17:1-8, Mark 9:2-8, Luke 9:28-36	Apparition, Outer locution, Ecstasy
The Annunciation	Luke 1:26-38	Apparition, Outer locution, Intellectual vision
Stephen's vision	Acts 7:55,56	Apparition
Philip's transport	Acts 8:39,40	Apparition, Intellectual vision
Saul's conversion	Acts 9:4-7	Apparition, Intellectual vision, Outer locution
Ananias' vision about Paul	Acts 9:10-16	Apparition, Intellectual vision, Outer locution
Cornelius' vision about Peter	Acts 10:3-8	Apparition, Intellectual vision, Outer locution
Peter's trance	Acts 10:10-16	Apparition, Intellectual vision
The Holy Spirit tells Peter about Cornelius' messengers	Acts 10:19-20	Outer locution, Intellectual vision
Peter's prison escape	Acts 12:7-11	Apparition, Imaginative vision
Barnabus and Paul selected for mission	Acts 13:2	Inner locution, Intellectual vision
Paul's vision of Macedonia	Acts 16:9	Apparition, Imaginative vision
Christ appears to Paul	Acts 18:9-10	Apparition
Agabus' trance	Acts 21:11	Imaginative vision
Paul's trance	Acts 22:17-21	Apparition, Intellectual vision
Christ appears to Paul again	Acts 23:11	Apparition, Intellectual vision
An angel appears to Paul before shipwreck	Acts 27:23,24	Apparition, Intellectual vision
A man's vision of the 3rd Heaven	2 Corinthians 12:2-4	Imaginative vision
John's trance and ecstasy	Revelation 1:10-20	Apparition, Imaginative vision, Inner locution

Table 2: New Testament Accounts of Paranormal Experiences

Please keep in mind that the references in Table 2 on the previous page are provided to give you a sample of legitimate Biblical methods of communication that God has used in the past to reveal things to His Church. The point here is that the apparition of Mary seems to be using orthodox, Biblical methods of revelation, too. That is all.

I realize that Table 2 may not be a complete list of paranormal occurrences, but I was surprised at the number of them, and all of these events fall into one category: extremely unusual. But they were from God, nonetheless. I included this table here to demonstrate exactly that point. We cannot disregard the occurrences of the apparition, or anything paranormal for that matter, based solely on our limited understanding of how God works. The truth is, He does work in mysterious ways. But that does not prove the apparitions are truly from God—it only proves that the apparitions are choosing to use methods of communication that are Biblical. The proof by which we discern the spirit behind them must be Biblical as well.

Tests

For if he that cometh preacheth another Jesus,
whom we have not preached, or if ye receive
another spirit, which ye have not received, or
another gospel, which ye have not accepted, ye
might well bear with him.
— *2 Corinthians 11:4*

I suppose that one of the problems with the New Age movement is that its adherents are so childishly unsuspecting. I know that this might seem to be a harsh thing to say, even hypocritical given Christ's instructions that we are to approach Him as a child would, and that no one can approach Him without becoming like one.[*] But the problem as I see it is that someone involved with the New Age movement might experience a genuine paranormal event and come to the conclusion that, "Since it is supernatural, it is therefore from God." Anyone who has read any of Shirley MacLaine's work will agree that she seems to place an unwarranted level of trust in things supernatural based solely on the fact that they occur.

But the Bible instructs us that beings in the spiritual realm are not to be trusted outright. As many Christians know, all things supernatural are not implicitly benevolent, regardless of outward appearances. Paul made that point clearly enough when he said that "Satan himself is transformed into an angel of light. Therefore it is no great thing if his ministers also be transformed as the ministers of righteousness."[56] As Christians, we should therefore know better than to accept all things as truth. We are to

---

[*] Matthew 18:3
[56] 2 Corinthians 11:14,15a

59

come to the Father as children, but as Christ instructed, while we are being as innocent as doves, we are also to be as shrewd as serpents.[*] And even doves know to stay away from their predators.

But if New Age believers suffer from one extreme of the problem, then Christians by far tend to suffer from the other. That is to say, while New Agers might describe a paranormal experience by saying, "It is supernatural, and therefore it is from God," a Christian might likewise describe the same paranormal experience by saying the converse: "It is not from God, and therefore it is not supernatural." This would thereby deny the reality of a legitimately, albeit evil, supernatural event. This is the theological equivalent of burying our collective head in the sand, and I believe that this is the way that the apparitions of Mary have been treated in Protestant circles.

The Pharisees had this same theology, and instead of coming to believe in the resurrection of Lazarus, they tried to kill the evidence: Lazarus himself.[†] Once, because of this theology, they came very near to committing the unpardonable sin and they blasphemed the Holy Spirit Who was at work in Christ.[§] And as long as the world's Christians continue to reject the apparitions of Mary based only on the fact that they seem strange to us, the followers of the apparitions will very justifiably accuse us of being modern-day Pharisees.

But if you think I wish to convince you to believe that the visions are from God, I may not have been clear in making my point. I do not wish to convince anyone that the apparitions find their source in Truth—I only wish to convince people that the apparitions are *really happening*. They are truly legitimate paranormal events which greatly need to be addressed by the Christian Church. But we cannot deny the authenticity of the apparitions of Mary simply because they seem awkward or out of the ordinary. There are better ways of proving their origins than by hiding ourselves behind a curtain of ignorance.

---

[*] Matthew 10:16
[†] John 12:10,11
[§] Matthew 12:22-32

I was surprised in my research to find that among the many hundreds of apparitions of Mary, only one° (to my knowledge) has yet been tested according to the Biblical method of testing the spirits. The proper test is revealed to us in 1 John 4:1-3a;

> "Beloved, believe not every spirit, but try the spirits whether they are of God: because many false prophets are gone out into the world. Hereby know ye the Spirit of God: Every spirit that confesseth that Jesus Christ is come in the flesh is of God: And every spirit that confesseth not that Jesus Christ is come in the flesh is not of God."

There are other criteria that a spirit must meet in addition to this test: its prophecies must come true[*] and it must teach the true Gospel which was delivered to the saints.[†] But 1 John 4 is the only Scripture which describes precisely the test of spirits. Curiously, it is this test that is consistently absent from any discussion on the apparitions, and the one apparition that was actually confronted in the manner described opted not to acknowledge Jesus Christ in the flesh, and instead changed the topic of conversation and then departed immediately.[§] But this is not to say that the rest of the apparitions have not been tested, for they have been tested, too. And by the most interesting means.

For example, when the apparition first appeared to the children of Medjugorje in 1981, they were understandably frightened. Any normal person would have been. So after the children had been receiving messages for a few days, they decided to make sure the apparitions were from God. When they returned the next day in anticipation of another vision of the woman, they brought with them a flask of holy water. When the woman appeared, Vicka (pronounced VEESH-ka) Ivankovic doused the apparition with the water. Marinko Ivankovic, a neighbor and friend of the visionaries, accompanied them that day. He explains:

° This apparition is addressed later in the chapter

[*] Deuteronomy 18:21,22

[†] Galatians 1:8,9

[§] This apparition is addressed later in the chapter

> "I had taken some holy water from my house to
> sprinkle around the vision in order to see what she is:
> Madonna, or devil. But when we had climbed up the
> hill and knelt down, I gave the holy water to Vicka."

Vicka explains what she did with it:

> "It was I who sprinkled the apparition, and I said in a
> loud voice, 'If you are Our Lady stay with us. If you
> are not her, leave us.' I went quite near her and did not
> spare the water. She smiled. I think she was
> pleased."[57]

When the children were later questioned as to whether or not
"Satan could pretend, and say, 'I am the Blessed Virgin Mary,'"
they responded that "they knew...that the devil would run away
from prayer and holy water."[58] This notion was later confirmed
by the apparition. It acknowledged their use of holy water as a
legitimate method of testing spirits and protecting against the evil
one, and even encouraged them to increase their use of it. This,
combined with the use of 'blessed objects,' would guarantee
protection against demons:

> "Carry blessed objects with you. Put them in your
> house, and restore the use of holy water... Dear
> children! Today I beg you to put more blessed objects
> in your homes, and that everyone carry blessed
> objects. Let every [object] be blessed so that Satan will
> tempt you less because you are armed against him."[59]

The apparitions at Medjugorje have yet to be officially
approved by the Church, but the test used there has its basis in the
method used to test an apparition that has been approved: the
apparition of Mary at Lourdes.

The story is that in 1858, young Bernadette Soubirous was
visited by the apparition of Mary while exploring the fields near

---

[57] Both quotes from "Between Heaven & Earth"

[58] Ashton, Joan, *The People's Madonna*, (London: Harper-Collins
Publishers, ©1991) pg. 179

[59] O'Carroll, Michael, CSSp, *Medjugorje: Facts, Documents, Theology*,
(Dublin, Ireland: Veritas Publications, ©1989) pp. 171,211. A message
from 1982, and the message of July 18, 1985. Brackets added for clarity

her home in Lourdes, France. A figure of a 'little lady' appeared to her that day while Bernadette's sister and friend were occupied with other pursuits in the fields nearby. When they returned, they found Bernadette kneeling before a shallow cave, or grotto, clutching a Rosary in her hands. They asked why she had been kneeling and she was initially silent on the matter, but later divulged the story which quickly spread around the small town. Two days later, Bernadette returned to the grotto accompanied by several friends,

> "...one of whom even carried in the pocket of her pinafore a little bottle secretly filled at the church with holy water to sprinkle over the 'little lady,' as Bernadette had now come to call her.
>
> "She herself arrived first at the grotto and when her young companions joined her she made them kneel down and take out their rosaries. The apparition kept the appointment that Bernadette had a feeling she intended to make, and towards the end of the first decade of the rosary, the child cried:
>
> "'There she is, she has a rosary over her right arm and she is looking at us!'
>
> "Bernadette... got up, took hold of the bottle of holy water, went towards the wild rose in the niche and cried out:
>
> "'If you come from God...stay!'
>
> "She threw the contents of the bottle over the 'lady' and instead of disappearing she smiled at Bernadette who, reassured, returned and knelt down among her friends."[60]

Since those visits of the apparition at Lourdes in 1858, countless miracles have taken place there, and many believers have attempted to document them in order to prove that Mary really visited Bernadette. Among them is Ruth Cranston, who records the following in her book, *The Miracle of Lourdes*:

> 'Thousands of spectators. Fifteen hundred sick in long double rows on the Esplanade—a large number of

---

[60] Agnellet, Michel, *I Accept These Facts*, (London: Max Parrish and Co. Ltd., ©1958) pp. 8-9. Trans. by John Dingle from the original *Cent Ans de Miracles a Lourdes*

> instantaneous cures. Among the sick who then arose
> from their stretchers and followed the Procession were
> Fanny Pepper, a consumptive in the last stages; Helene
> Duval, tubercular peritonitis; Philimene Albrecht,
> Pott's Disease; Josephine Grosset, tuberculous peri-
> tonitis; Irma Jacquart, cerebral affection complicated
> by paralysis; Felicie Serreau, another peritonitis
> victim; J. Lacome, Pott's Disease...'"[61]

More than 60 other official cures are documented in detail in
Appendix E of Cranston's book,[62] and her desire to authenticate
the origins of the apparitions is truly admirable. The same can be
said of the children in their use of holy water. But these tests only
prove that the apparitions can withstand a sprinkling of holy
water, and that something visited Bernadette at Lourdes in 1858
and still works miracles today. But for all of their sincerity of
heart, Cranston and the visionaries have proven nothing at all
about the origins of the apparitions.

Another example of other-than-Biblical methods of testing
the spirits is that of the apparition occurring daily in a small town
just southeast of Atlanta, Georgia, USA. The town is called
Conyers, and the apparition has been appearing there since 1987
to a woman named Nancy Fowler. Often a spirit identifying itself
as Jesus appears with the apparition of Mary, and to make sure
that Nancy keeps herself from being deceived, the two spirits
have given her a strict method of testing their authenticity:

> "Nancy is under obedience to Jesus and Our Loving
> Mother to test all messages and appearances because
> Jesus has told her that 'My elect children all over the
> world are being deceived.' One test is to throw Holy
> Water on the image. Another is for Jesus to identify
> Himself by saying, 'I am Jesus. I bow down to God.
> To Him alone I give the glory and honor.'
>
> "Very often, Our Loving Mother will identify
> Herself before She begins speaking to help Nancy test
> the authenticity of the vision. 'I am the Blessed Virgin
> Mary, the Holy Mother of God and Your Loving

---

[61] Cranston, Ruth, *The Miracle of Lourdes*, (New York: Doubleday &
Company, Inc., ©1955, 1983, 1988) pg. 261. Cranston quotes from one
Dr. Vallet, an eyewitness to the events described here.

[62] Cranston, pp. 339-51

Mother. I bow down to God the Father. I adore, I worship, I love Him with my whole heart, mind and soul and all my strength. Jesus is the Son of God and I serve Him.' Once when asked to test the message by saying, 'The Blessed Virgin is greater than Satan,' Our Loving Mother corrected the statement by saying, 'By the grace of God, the Blessed Virgin Mary is greater than Satan.'"[63]

And on another occasion, Nancy administered another test:

"Nancy asked, 'Please, Jesus, identify Yourself.' Jesus said, 'I am Jesus. I am one with the Father. I am the Second Person of the Blessed Trinity. I am He who speaks to you.'"[64]

All of these tests notwithstanding, Nancy has yet to prove that the apparitions of Mary and of Jesus are from God. She has yet to use the Biblical test, and has only proven to this point that the spirits with whom she communicates can make statements and allegations which demons are perfectly capable of making anyway.

In another case, that of the apparitions in Garabandal, Spain, from 1961 to 1965, the priest at a local parish was skeptical of the apparitions that the visionaries there were experiencing. So in order to determine that the apparitions were genuine, he performed a test involving the use of a crucifix:

"That very day, a totally skeptical priest from Asturias arrived wearing street clothes. He watched one of the children approach him. She offered him a crucifix to kiss several times. 'If this is genuine,' he thought to himself, 'let the child come to.' In an instant the visionary emerged from her ecstasy, smiled at the priest and turned to go home. Hardly had she taken a few steps, when she again went into a trance. The priest then said to himself: 'If you've just made the Sign of the Cross over me with your crucifix because I am a priest, I want you to prove it to me again, giving me the crucifix to kiss and crossing me several times.'

---

[63] *To Bear Witness,* pp. 6-7

[64] *To Bear Witness,* pg. 95, para. 160. Message of December 29, 1990

...No sooner had this request formed in his mind than
the child turned round, came to him, 'smiled, and besides proffering me the crucifix to kiss, made the Sign
of the Cross over me three times in succession.'"[65]

But the priest's tests accomplished nothing, save to prove that
the apparition was capable of reading his mind and causing the
visionary to make the sign of the cross. It did not prove divine
origins.

Perhaps the most intriguing miracle to prove that an
apparition was from God was that given by the apparition at
Fátima, Portugal in 1917. At one of the occurrences of the Fátima
apparition, Lucia Abóbora inquired of it, "What is it you want of
me?" The apparition replied,

"I want you to continue to go to Cova da Iria on the
thirteenth day and to continue to recite the Rosary
every day. In the last month I will perform a miracle
so that all shall believe."

The last month finally came, and William Thomas Walsh
reports what happened in his book, *Our Lady of Fátima*. In the
middle of a clear blue sky over Fátima that day, 70,000 spectators
saw the sun begin to spin, change to all the colors of the rainbow
in succession and then hurl "blood-red streamers of flame" across
the sky. Finally, the sun did something completely unheard of, not
to mention astrophysically impossible:

"Madly gyrating in this manner three times, the fiery
orb seemed to tremble, to shudder, and then to plunge
precipitately, in a mighty zigzag, toward the crowd...
This had lasted about ten minutes, perhaps. Then all
saw the sun begin to climb, in the same zigzag
manner, to where it had appeared before. It became
tranquil, then dazzling. No one could look at it any
longer. It was the sun of every day. ...As early as May,
1917, Jacinta and Lucia had told people that the Lady
they saw had promised a miracle on October 13, at the
hour of noon, as a sign of their sincerity. ...On the very
day and hour they had foretold, some 70,000 persons

---

[65] Sanchez-Ventura y Pascual, F., *The Apparitions of Garabandal*, (MI:
San Miguel Publishing Co., ©1966) pg. 88

testified that they had the unique experience of seeing
the sun spin round and seem to fall."[66]

This phenomenon, called 'The Miracle of the Sun' or 'The
Dance of the Sun' by the faithful, has happened at many locations
of Marian apparitions, from Medjugorje, Bosnia, to Lubbock,
Texas and Conyers, Georgia, USA, to Sabana Grande, Puerto
Rico. And according to the visionaries, "Our Lady said these are
all signs for us to believe more—that all those who see them may
believe better."[67]

Granted, these are admirable, even mind-boggling feats for
the apparitions to perform in order to guarantee that they are
whom they claim to be, but identifying oneself as Mary does not
make someone Mary, and identifying oneself as Jesus Christ does
not make someone Jesus Christ. Many people have tried that
before, and still do. Offering a crucifix to someone does not prove
divine origins, and sprinkling a vision with holy water does not
force a demon to speak truthfully. Commanding an apparition to
leave if it is not Mary is completely useless as a method for
discerning spirits, and making the sun come down to earth while
70,000 people look on is truly fascinating, but it doesn't prove a
thing about the origins of the apparition. It only proves that it
exists. But even if something looks like Mary, acts like Mary and
says it is Mary, all of the claims, miracles and cures don't mean
anything if it isn't really her. And if a spirit identifies itself as
Jesus, what does that matter if it isn't truly Him?

Jesus warned that many would come claiming to be Him, but
that we should not allow ourselves to be deceived:

> "Take heed that ye be not deceived: for many shall
> come in my name, saying, I am Christ; and the time
> draweth near: go ye not therefore after them."[68]

I bring this up only to point out that spirits which are not from
God are capable of identifying themselves as Jesus Christ, as

---

[66] Walsh, William Thomas, *Our Lady of Fátima*, (New York:
Doubleday & Company, Inc., ©1947, 1954) pp. 145-6,50
[67] "Medjugorje: The Lasting Sign," a video narrated by Martin Sheen.
Directed by Rob Wallace. Produced by Cinematic Visions, Inc., ©1989,
All Rights Reserved. Visionary referenced is Marija Pavlovic
[68] Luke 21:8. See also Matthew 24:4,5

Mary, or anything good, even when put to the test, *as long as it is
not a Biblical method of testing them.*

Consider the story of Johanna Michaelsen. Before she became
a Christian she was very heavily involved in the occult—
spiritism, divining, clairvoyance, psychic surgery—she was
completely immersed in it. And she had a spirit guide, or
ascended master, with whom she would consult regularly. He
called himself Jesus, and she met him during a four-day mind
control training seminar called "Applied ESP." Johanna recorded
these events in her book, *The Beautiful Side of Evil,* and she
explains what happened when she was first introduced to her
counselor in her psychic laboratory after a descent into Alpha
level consciousness:

> "As my door came down, the room was filled
> with a radiant light that emanated from the figure
> standing behind it. Slowly, an inch at a time, the figure
> emerged. Shimmering brown hair parted in the middle,
> a high forehead, dark skin; eyes brown, deep and
> gentle. There! It was Jesus! The door went down now
> of its own accord, revealing the rest of the figure
> which was robed in a long white linen garment. He
> was glowing with a holy radiance and smiling softly. I
> stood, then fell at his feet."[69]

One could hardly deny that the visions or encounters Johanna
was experiencing seemed to be with Jesus, and the spirit with
whom she was dealing consented *by its appearance* to the belief
in Jesus Christ, even His bodily incarnation and deity. But it was
still an evil spirit. Johanna was never able to discern that until
much later after she became Christian and learned of the Biblical
method for testing spirits. What happened when she used it is
fascinating:

> "It was during a time of prayer shortly after this
> that it occured(sic) to me to test the spirits according to
> I John 4:1. I went into my [psychic] laboratory and
> summoned my counselors.

---

[69] Taken from *The Beautiful Side of Evil*, by Johanna Michaelsen,
pp. 74-5. Copyright ©1982 by Johanna Michaelsen. Used by permission.
Published by Harvest House Publishers, Eugene, Oregon 97402

> "'You are not the Jesus in the Bible, are you,' I
> challenged the figure of 'Jesus' which stood before me
> in the shadows. There was no reply. His eyes were
> closed... 'Then I command you in the Name of Jesus
> Christ of Nazareth, tell me: Do you believe that Jesus
> Christ is God uniquely incarnate in human flesh?' A
> violent flash—as though from a powerful bomb,
> brought the walls of my amethyst and gold laboratory
> down all around me. When I looked up, my counselors
> had vanished."[70]

If this really happened, and I am persuaded that it did, it is
worthwhile to note that even a spirit appearing as Jesus was
thoroughly unable to acknowledge a question to which an
affirmative answer was the only obvious response. Given this
description of Johanna's encounter, it is interesting that the
methods used by the children at Lourdes and Medjugorje, by the
priest at Garabandal, and those methods prescribed by the
apparition at Conyers and Medjugorje never once resemble that
given in the Bible. They have yet to use—or prescribe—the
method that the Bible prescribes and which Johanna Michaelsen
used so successfully. As Johanna's situation clearly demonstrates,
even the demons believe in Jesus Christ,* sometimes appearing in
the likeness of Him, but that only proves that they are able to
deceive by appearing as angels of light and ministers of the
righteousness of God.

In other attempts to validate the apparitions, some enthusiasts
have gone to different extremes to prove that they are real by
using purely scientific methods. One case that comes to mind is
the test done on the children of Medjugorje, at which time
electrodes were placed at various locations on their bodies while
they were actually having an apparition. With all the electrical
equipment attached, the children fell to their knees simultaneously
and began to participate in what seemed like a one-sided
conversation—their lips moving, but silent. The most convincing
proof, aside from the simultaneous drop to their knees, was the
fact that all of their eye movements, after being quite random and
independent before the apparition began, were very much in

---

[70] Michaelsen, pg. 154. Brackets added for clarity. Used by permission
* James 2:19

synch with each other during the vision. The electronic equipment attached to the six children indicated that all of their eyes focused on the same point within 0.2 second,[71] and if the numbers don't convince you, the video footage would. Seeing the visionaries acting very much like children and then immediately dropping to their knees as though someone else had pushed them there, gave the chilling impression that someone else actually had.

Similar, if not more disturbing footage is available from Garabandal, Spain. It shows Conchita González and her friend walking around in an ecstatic trance during an apparition. They seemed to care nothing of any obstacles in their way and were undaunted by the inconvenience, not to mention discomfort, of walking around on their knees, or backwards without looking where they were going. All of this on a rocky, graveled path, without injury while their faces were directed nearly straight upward in a position that even young, flexible children should have found uncomfortable. They were constantly raising religious articles to an unseen person, apparently to have each article blessed and kissed by the apparition of Mary, and occasionally even lifted each other with no effort at all for the same purpose. At a later time Conchita was promised a miracle, during which an apparition of St. Michael the Archangel, who was appearing in concert with the apparition of Mary, would place a host (Eucharistic wafer) on her tongue so that people would believe he was appearing to her. Although the apparition of St. Michael was invisible, the wafer was not, and it was captured on film to prove beyond a doubt that someone had actually placed a piece of bread on Conchita's tongue.[72] And I don't doubt that someone did.

The trance that these children experienced in Garabandal is similar to that experienced by Nancy Fowler during her apparitions in Conyers, Georgia, USA. Nancy's trances were tested

---

[71] Laurentin, René, and Henri Joyeux, *Scientific & Medical Studies on the Apparitions at Medjugorje*, (Dublin, Ireland: Veritas Publications, ©1987) pg. 66

[72] "Marian Apparitions of the 20th Century: A Message of Urgency," a video narrated by Ricardo Montalban. Produced and written by Drew J. Mariani and Anne McGeehan-McGlone. Directed by Drew J. Mariani. Produced at the Eternal Word Television Network, Birmingham, AL. Marian Communications, Ltd., ©1991, International Copyrights Reserved

recently by a team of experts which included Ricardo Castanon, a professor of neuropsychophysiology at the Catholic University of Bolivia, two neurologists, two EEG technicians, a psychiatrist, a retired research scientist from the University of Florida and Umberto Velasquez, a radiation scientist from the Florida State Department of Health. The purpose of the team was to determine if there was any physical evidence for the supernatural encounters Nancy was describing. Their findings were extraordinary. Using an instrument that measures the electrical conductivity of the subject's skin, it was determined that Nancy was indeed having a supernatural encounter:

> "Professor Castanon said that at the beginning of the tests, Nancy had a reading of between 1.5 and 1.7 millivolts reflecting anxiety. But once she began to pray, she instantly produced a reading of 0.2 millivolts. This reading of 0.2 millivolts represents a most complete state of relaxation and cannot be normally achieved in the way Nancy did. During the apparition at noon on June 13, Nancy produced a reading of 0.2 millivolts, but at 12:25:05 the reading was nil which indicated to him that her brain had stopped functioning. He found this inexplicable because Nancy was awake, alert and communicating to others what she was experiencing. He was convinced that his instruments remained in working order. This occurred one second, at 12:25:04, before Dr. Sanchez's EEG recorded an artifact or unique brain activity of Nancy going from an awake state to the state of someone in a deep slep(sic) or coma."

This evidence of course proved that something was really happening to Nancy during the apparition, but another test indicated that a foreign presence was actually in the room and interacting with her at the time of the test:

> "On June 13, 1993 throughout the time Nancy said that the Virgin Mary was appearing to her, one could hear a beeping sound coming from the radiation detecting instrument that Mr. Velasquez was using. He later confirmed that from the time Nancy said that the Virgin Mary had appeared to the time she said she had

left, he detected the presence of ionized radiation in
the room. He could not explain why that happened."[73]

These tests were just a few of the many psychological,
physiological and neurological tests that were performed that day
and all of them offer proof that Nancy Fowler is completely
normal—as far as the experiments were able to determine
normality. Additionally, the tests provided evidence that something visited Nancy Fowler in the parlor of her home that day.
And for my part I don't doubt that something did.

In the case of the apparition in Akita, Japan, a statue of Mary
was known to cry tears on more than 100 separate occasions,
seemingly to confirm the authenticity of the messages being
received from Mary when she appeared to Sister Sasagawa. At
one point the tears were collected by Bishop John Ito, then-
Ordinary of the Diocese of Niigata, and analyzed at a leading
Japanese university, whereupon they were determined to be real,
human tears.[74] And I don't doubt that they were.

And I wouldn't have needed the chemical, neurological and
physiological tests or the video footage for proof, either. The
simple fact is that something is appearing, frequently to children
and increasingly to adults, in many places around the world. And
whatever it is has been deceiving them through signs and
wonders, and has been masquerading as Christ Himself, His
mother Mary, and sometimes as Michael the Archangel to do it.

But merely appearing as Jesus Christ, or any other Biblical
character for that matter, does not constitute a valid demonstration
of spiritual origins, and evidence of the paranormal is not
evidence of the divine. You may notice that in 1 John 4:1-3a, the
test was not designed to prove paranormality. The passage
presumes that much and then goes on to help the believers discern
the origins of the spirit that is appearing. But only Biblical
methods of testing the spirits will be successful in discerning
whether or not a spirit is from God. To date, no such methods
have been used by the visionaries, and Biblical methods for the

---

[73] Both quotes from *The Journal of Reported Teachings and Messages
from Our Lord and Our Loving Mother*, July 1994 issue, compiled by
Our Loving Mother's Children, Conyers, GA, 30207. "Overview of the
Medical and Scientific Testing," pp. 2-3
[74] "Marian Apparitions of the 20th Century: A Message of Urgency"

most part have been avoided by the apparitions themselves. We must ask at this time a question which practically asks itself: if the apparition were truly Mary, why wouldn't she recommend Biblical tests, and why would she avoid these tests so consistently?

As mentioned earlier, there is one apparition to date that has actually recommended the Biblical test of spirits. That apparition appears regularly to Maureen Hinko of Seven Hills, Ohio, USA. Maureen's description of what happened when she used the test is most interesting because when the test was applied, the apparition changed the topic of conversation, rambled for a few lines and then departed without ever answering Maureen's question—and certainly without ever acknowledging Jesus in the flesh:

> "I said, 'Do you believe Jesus was born of the flesh?' She [responded], 'I am the Mother of the Word Incarnate. Do you understand, my daughter, my words to you lay bare the path of holiness to my Heart and the Heart of my Son for His remnant flock? It is through holy love that you will be signs of joy and peace in times of adversity. You cannot trust if you do not first love.' Our Lady blessed me and left."[75]

In short, the apparition did nothing more than continue to assert what it had from the beginning: that it was Jesus' mother, something that demons can claim anyway. The apparition merely acknowledged that it was Mary, which is what every apparition acknowledges and which certainly wasn't the question. The test was never repeated and the visionary did not force the issue, no doubt to the relief of the apparition.

In another case, a spirit claiming to be Jesus, acting in concert with another claiming to be Mary, actually recommended against the test in 1 John 4:2, and suggested a better method of discerning the spirits—one that didn't require a direct confrontation:

> "Dear children, it is very good always to test the spirits, but in Scripture I have told you the one true

---

[75] *Holy Love: Messages from Our Blessed Mother Leading Souls to Holiness*, (Seven Hills, OH: Holy Love Ministries, ©1994) pp. 32-33. Message of September 21, 1993. Brackets added for clarity

and infallible way to do this: 'By their fruits, you shall know them.'"[76]

The spirit identifying itself as Jesus refers to the well known passage of Matthew 7:16 which is a test of *prophets*, not a test of spirits, and is not the 'one true and infallible' test. We can safely assume that Jesus would not err in a reference to Scripture, and therefore we must presume that the spirit was not whom it claimed to be and that it had a vested interest in making sure that the proper test was not applied. The infallible test of spirits that Scripture really reveals to us is located in 1 John 4—a test that is systematically discouraged and avoided by the apparitions. This fear of being properly tested is prevalent in the many messages given by the apparitions, and explains, to some degree, why their followers prefer to accept the apparition based solely on its own authority without testing it at all. The followers of the Medjugorje apparition write:

> "Her words do not exaggerate and we do not have to debate whether Our Lady is right or wrong."[77]

But we **do**. The Bible tells us so.

And the standards by which the apparitions must be measured are found in the same Book that instructs us to test them. We must use Biblical methods, like the one in 1 John 4, and not only have the apparitions been reluctant to use that test in the manner prescribed, but they have shown themselves at least once to be unable just to answer the question when it is asked. But if the apparitions will not answer a simple question when it is put to them, then there is one more test by which the origin of a spirit may be determined:

The Gospel of Jesus Christ.

---

[76] *A Call to Peace*, Volume 4, Number 1. Published by MIR-A-CALL Center, Bella Vista, Arkansas, Michael Cain, editor. "1992 Locutions from the Hidden Flower of the Immaculate Heart," pg. 4. Message of January 23, 1992

[77] *Understanding Our Lady's Messages*, pg. 9

Part II Salve Regina

Hail, holy Queen, Mother of Mercy, our life, our sweetness and our hope. To thee do we cry, poor banished children of Eve. To thee do we send up our sighs, mourning and weeping in this valley of tears. Turn then, most gracious advocate, thine eyes of mercy towards us. And after this our exile, show unto us the blessed Fruit of thy womb, Jesus. O clement, O loving, O sweet Virgin Mary. Pray for us, O holy Mother of God that we may be made worthy of the promises of Christ. Amen.

—The Hail, Holy Queen

Redemptress

> But though we, or an angel from heaven, preach
> any other gospel unto you than that which we have
> preached unto you, let him be accursed
> —*Galatians 1:8*

ONE of the clearest Old Testament references to Christ can be found in Isaiah 53. There are others, but I do not wish to develop a complex theological argument here. I only wish to demonstrate that God offered Christ as an atoning sacrifice for our sins, and that all of our sins were placed on Him. This is a very simple Biblical concept, and I do not wish to complicate it with my own exposition. I will let the Word speak for itself:

> "Surely he hath borne our griefs,
>   and carried our sorrows:
> Yet we did esteem him stricken,
>   smitten of God, and afflicted.
> But he was wounded for our transgressions,
>   he was bruised for our iniquities:
> The chastisement of our peace was upon him;
>   and with his stripes we are healed.
> All we like sheep have gone astray; we have turned
> every one to his own way; and the LORD hath laid on
> him the iniquity of us all."[78]

Now, I realize that this is a very straightforward passage and the only way I could make it less so would be to attempt to explain it, so I won't. But try as I might, there is one thing I

---

[78] Isaiah 53:4-6

cannot do. In searching this passage, or any other passage like it in the whole Bible, I cannot find anything that says our sins were placed on anyone else but Christ alone. Not on Moses, nor any of the prophets, nor any of the apostles,[*] nor any of the disciples. I cannot find a single passage in Scripture that says my sins were placed even on myself—only on Christ. By the grace of God, my sins rested on His shoulders at Calvary, and are no longer given to my account. Jesus suffered in my place for my sins. He died in my place for my sins. He paid for my sins with His own blood instead of mine. And in spite of bearing the burden of my punishment, the curse of death, He rose again three days later. Since He did all of this, I have no reason to place my trust in anyone else. Nor do I have any reason to feel remorse that anyone else besides Jesus had to pay the price for my sins and suffer for them in my place. The price that needed to be paid for my sin was paid by Jesus Christ, and "there is no more offering for sin."[79]

I do not wish to belabor the point any further, but I did want to set the stage for what you are about to read. What follows is a catalog of reports and messages that have been quoted from apparitions of Mary around the world and throughout history. They portray a suffering savior who is burdened with the weight of our sins, whose blood purges us of our guilt. They portray a redemptress whose pain relieves us from the guilt of our disobedience: Mary.

Apparition of Mary to the children of Medjugorje, Bosnia 1981-present

> "I love you even when you are far away from me and my Son. I ask you not to allow my heart to shed tears of blood because of the souls who are being lost through sin."[80]

---

[*] Curiously, Paul's words in Colossians 1:24 are sometimes taken to mean exactly that, for he says, "and fill up that which is behind of the afflictions of Christ in my flesh for his body's sake." However, the only times that Paul actually reveals what it is that his sufferings are accomplishing (Phil. 1:12-18, 2 Tim. 2:8-10, etc.), he makes it clear that his sufferings always resulted in the *preaching* of the Gospel, which was in fact the only thing that was lacking at the cross.(Romans 10:14-15)

[79] Hebrews 10:18

[80] O'Carroll, pg. 161. Message of May 24, 1984

Apparition of Mary to Julia Kim, Naju, South Korea
1985-present

"I pray without ceasing for those of my children who
have fallen into vice and corruption, suffering in their
place."[81]

Apparition of Mary to Sister Agnes Sasagawa, Akita, Japan
1973-1981

"...a bleeding wound appeared on the right hand of the
statue of Our Lady in the chapel. Sister's guardian
angel told her the flowing of blood is significant for
the conversion of sinners and in reparation for sins."[82]

Apparition of Mary to Lucia Abóbora, Fátima, Portugal
1917

"'Jesus wishes to make use of you to have me
acknowledged and loved. He wishes to establish in the
world the devotion to My Immaculate Heart' ..[Lucia
recalled,] 'Before the palm of the right hand of Our
Lady was a Heart encircled by thorns which seemed to
have pierced it like nails. We understood that it was
the Immaculate Heart of Mary outraged by the sins of
humanity, for which there must be reparation.'"[83]

Apparition of Mary to Sister Mary of Agreda, Spain
circa 1617

"The great Mother humiliated Herself to the lowest
depths; ...She bewailed the universal forgetfulness and
want of appreciation of the blood shed for the rescue
of all. And, as if ashamed in the presence of her divine
Son for not having paid her debts, She offered her own
life and her own blood in satisfaction and in imitation

---

[81] "Marian Apparitions of the 20th Century: A Message of Urgency"
[82] "Marian Apparitions of the 20th Century: A Message of Urgency"
[83] Walsh, *Our Lady of Fátima*, pp. 68-9. Brackets added for clarity

of her Master's example. ...She begged that She alone
be singled out to suffer for his love."[84]

Apparition of Mary to Nancy Fowler, Conyers, Georgia, USA 1987-present

"Our Loving Mother said, 'We are both revealing our
suffering faces to you. Tell others we suffer for them
in love.'"[85]

"During the vision, Jesus appeared to Nancy on the
cross and, then, merged with an image of His Mother.
This vision was repeated over and over and over and
over. The vision appeared to show the oneness of their
suffering."[86]

"The people, and you, yesterday received very special
graces. It is very rare that my Son grants permission to
see my suffering face."[87]

Apparition of Mary to Tarcisio di Biasi, Oliveto Citra, Italy 1985

"My son, when you recite the rosary, you should think
that in each mystery there is contained all the love and
suffering of my Son and of myself for all of you."[88]

Apparition of Mary to Juan Angel Collado, Sabana Grande, Puerto Rico 1953

"The indifference of the children of God will not allow
them to see the great danger which lies in wait. The
pain in my heart will be all the more piercing, since it
will be these especially beloved sons who abandon

---

[84] Mary of Agreda, *Mystical City of God*, Volume IV, *The Coronation*, pg. 565, para. 666

[85] *To Bear Witness*, pg. 99, para. 172. Message of February 2, 1991

[86] *To Bear Witness*, pg. 68, para. 86. Vision of March 29, 1991

[87] *To Bear Witness*, pg. 68, para. 89. Message of March 30, 1991

[88] *Our Lady Queen of Peace*, "Our Lady in Italy," pg. 14. Message of
May 7, 1986. Used by permission

me... The selfishness of the children of God will be the cause of conflicts and divisions which will intensify my pain."[89]

Apparition of Mary to Maximin Giraud and Melanie Mathieu, LaSalette, France
1846

"For a long time I have suffered for you; if I do not want my son to abandon you, I am forced to pray to him myself without ceasing. You pay no heed. However much you would do, you could never recompense the pain I have taken for you."[90]

These are only a few of the many quotes I have been able to locate. There are many more that describe Mary's suffering and the blood she sheds for us, but the issue is hardly one of a need for suffering. It is clearly established in the Scriptures that payment is needed to make reparation for sin. The real issue is one of Who it is that is worthy to pay the price for our sin by suffering for us. We needed Someone to suffer and die in our place, to pay the price for our rebellion and take away the burden of our sins.

Only Jesus can.

Only Jesus did.

The apparition of Mary and its cohorts are not at all who they claim to be. They are teaching a false gospel.

---

[89] *Our Lady Queen of Peace*, "Our Lady of the Rosary in Puerto Rico," pg. 13. Message of April, 1953. Used by permission
[90] Zimdars-Swartz, pg. 30. Message of September 19, 1846

Mediatrix

I am the way, the truth, and the life: no man
cometh unto the Father, but by me.
—*John 14:6*b

AMONG Christians, it is a fundamentally and universally understood precept of the Gospel that men and women everywhere are naturally separated from God and need to be reconciled to Him. Because of the sin nature passed on to each of us through the bloodline of Adam, we are in need of being restored to the privilege that Adam and Eve enjoyed: that of oneness with the Creator. As a result of the barrier, a gap, that has been erected because of Adam's sin, we no longer have free access to the throne of God. But God solved the problem. The barrier which was too big, the gulf that spanned the infinity between God and man, the distance that was so incomprehensibly large that man could not traverse it, has been broken down, traversed, by one Person, Jesus Christ. Because we could not possibly travel the great distance that was necessarily placed between Him and ourselves by Adam's rebellion against Him, He had to travel the distance for us. In doing so, He willingly forfeited what was rightfully His and became like us. Upon Him was placed the very worst of us, in order that we might have what only He was worthy of having:

> "For he hath made him to be sin for us, who knew no sin; that we might be made the righteousness of God in him."[91]

---

[91] 2 Corinthians 5:21

In performing this greatest act of love, Christ placed Himself between a Righteous God and sinful man, and henceforth He acts as a Mediator between us. It is not possible for us to go directly to the Father—our sin prevents that. But we *can* approach Jesus, the Mediator, and He can approach God on our behalf. He can plead our case before the Father and reconcile us to Him. As it is written,

> "Wherefore he is able also to save them to the uttermost that come unto God by him, seeing he ever liveth to make intercession for them."[92]

There is no need for me to expound on this any further. The Word speaks for itself.

But in all my studies, I have been thoroughly unable to find a passage of Scripture that indicates that there is another mediator, that there is someone else who can go before God on my behalf. Not Moses, nor any of the prophets, nor any of the apostles, nor any of the disciples. I have not discovered anywhere in Scripture that I can place my trust in anyone but Jesus Christ to act as Mediator between me and the God I rebelled against. And I can find nothing to show that I need *another* mediator between me and Jesus, the true and only Way to the Father.

I do not wish to belabor this point any further either, but I did want to set the stage for what you are about to read. What follows is a catalog of messages which have been quoted from apparitions of Mary and apparitions of Jesus around the world and throughout history. They portray a merciful mediatrix, who is gracefully placing herself between sinful man and an Angry Jesus. Between sinful man and a Righteous God. They portray a loving, caring mediatrix through whom we may approach a Holy Jesus, and through whom we can be reconciled to the Father: Mary.

Apparition of Mary to the children of Medjugorje, Bosnia 1981-present

> "I invite you to prayer so that you may meet God... For this reason, little children, set aside a time during the day to pray in peace and humility, to have this

---

[92] Hebrews 7:25

encounter with God the Creator. I am with you and I
intercede greatly before God."[93]

"Today I invite you to reflect on why I am so long
with you. I am a Mediatress between you and God."[94]

Apparition of Mary to Patricia Talbot, El Cajas, Ecuador 1988-present

"I am holding back the hand of my son; and if my
children convert, the Heart of my son will soften; and
the intensity can be diminished or lost forever. If not,
the great trial will come."[95]

Apparition of Mary to Nancy Fowler, Conyers, Georgia, USA 1987-present

"...the sins of this country and the sins of the world are
increasing God's anger. Please tell my children. Please
tell my children, come back to God. Return from their
wicked, evil ways. I cannot restrain His arm much
longer. Please—Please—Please listen."[96]

"I am receiving the petitions from your heart. I am
receiving them in my heart and giving them to the
heart of Jesus."[97]

Apparition of Mary to Gladys Quiroga de Motta, San Nicolás, Argentina 1983-1990

"Truly, this time is a precious time. It should not be
wasted, but one should profit from it, for the
Redeemer offers humanity the way of confronting
death, which is only Satan, as He did it after the Cross.

[93] O'Carroll, pp. 224-5. Message of November 25, 1988

[94] O'Carroll, pg. 181. Message of July 17, 1986

[95] *Our Lady Queen of Peace*, "An Urgent Call to Mankind," pg. 1.
Message of September 1, 1988. Used by permission

[96] *To Bear Witness*, pg. 97, para. 167. Message of April 15, 1991

[97] *To Bear Witness*, pg. 74, para. 105. Message of February 13, 1991

He also offers it His own Mother; Mediatrix of all graces."[98]

Apparition of Jesus to Nancy Fowler, Conyers, Georgia, USA 1987-present

"Look from where graces flow, where they start. If there were no graces from Me, there would be no one on earth. My graces flow through My Mother. Now I am giving you My graces."[99]

"I come through My Mother and I want you, dear children, to come through My Mother on your journey back to Me."[100]

"Stand against My Mother and you stand against Me. If you do not accept My Mother then you are dismembered from Me. Did you hear what [name]* said of My Mother's position? He placed her in the neck. I like that position. Tell others about this. When they cut My Mother off, they are cutting the neck. Remove the neck; remove My Mother. Then you are dead. Then you are completely dismembered from My body."[101]

Apparition of Mary to Theresa Lopez, Denver, Colorado, USA 1991-present

"I tell you again, I am your mother, your intercessor with my Son. I need prayers from the heart to grant these requests all the people of the nations call to me for. I desire to offer your prayers to my Son."[102]

---

[98] *Our Lady Queen of Peace*, "An Urgent Appeal: Our Lady in Argentina," pg. 7. Message of January 5, 1987. Used by permission
[99] *To Bear Witness*, pg. 63, para. 73. Message of August 26, 1990
[100] *To Bear Witness*, pg. 66, para. 80. Message of February 10, 1991
* The person's name was omitted here in the original
[101] *To Bear Witness*, pg. 64, para. 75. Message of December 4, 1990
[102] Kuntz, J. Gary, *Our Holy Mother of Virtues: Messages for the Harvest*, Volume 1, (Denver, CO: Colorado MIR Center, ©1992) pg. 42. Message of February 11, 1991

"I ask you to pray and ask boldly from me. I will
intercede in front of God for you."[103]

Apparition of Mary to Beulah Lynch, Bessbrook Grotto, Ireland
1987

"My child, I am your mother, Mother of God. You
cannot know the wrath of God. God is very, very
angry because of the sins of the world. I cannot hold
back any longer."[104]

Apparition of Mary to Lucia Abóbora, Fátima, Portugal
1917

"I will never forsake you. My Immaculate Heart will
be your refuge and the road that will conduct you to
God."[105]

Apparition of Mary to Maria Esperanza Bianchini, Betania, Venezuela
1984

"My children I am Mary, Virgin Mother of
reconciliation of people and nations and I come with
my son in arms to reconcile you... oh sublime hope for
all, pray the rosary."[106]

Apparition of Mary to Pierina Gilli, Montichiari, Italy
1947

"I have place(sic) myself as the mediatrix between my
Divine Son and mankind, especially for the souls
consecrated to God."[107]

---

[103] Kuntz, pg. 43. Message of February 23, 1991

[104] *Our Lady Queen of Peace*, "Apparitions Europe," pg. 11. Message
of November 11, 1987. Used by permission

[105] Walsh, *Our Lady of Fátima*, pg. 68

[106] *Our Lady Queen of Peace*, "In Venezuela, Bishop Approves
Apparitions," pg. 12. Message of March 25, 1984. Used by permission

[107] *Our Lady Queen of Peace*, "Mystical Rose: Mother of the Church,"
pg. 17. Message of October 22, 1947. Used by permission

Apparition of Mary to Maximin Giraud and Melanie Mathieu, LaSalette, France
1846

> "If my people will not obey I shall be compelled to loose my Son's arm. It is so heavy, so pressing that I can no longer restrain it."[108]

These are only a few of the quotes I have been able to locate. There are many more, but the issue is not one of a need for mediation—rather it is an issue of Whom it is that is worthy to mediate for us. We need someone to do this between us and the God we rebelled against, and even if Mary wanted to stay the wrath of her Son, she couldn't. Even if she wanted to hold back the anger of God, she would crumble under His mighty hand. She doesn't have the power to withstand the righteous anger of the Father. We need Someone Who does. We need Someone to lead us to God, and to protect us from His just and holy wrath.

Only Jesus can.

Only Jesus does.

The apparition of Mary and its cohorts are not at all who they claim to be. They are teaching a false gospel.

---

[108] Lord, Bob & Penny, *The Many Faces of Mary: A Love Story*, (Westlake Village, CA: Journeys of Faith, ©1987) , pg. 70. Message of September 19, 1846

High Priestess

> For every high priest is ordained to offer gifts and sacrifices: wherefore it is of necessity that this man have somewhat also to offer.
> —*Hebrews 8:3*

THERE was a time before Christ when it was prescribed by the Law of Moses that one man of the Tribe of Levi should be designated as high priest. Every year this high priest would enter into the Holy of Holies to offer a sacrifice—a sacrifice which could never take away sins.* The sacrifices which he offered year after year only served as a reminder of our perpetual slavery to sin—a bondage from which only Christ Himself could free us. And in accordance with the Law, the perfect High Priest, Jesus Christ, came and offered up a Sacrifice that would once and for all take away the sin of the world. He offered the only sacrifice that could truly be pleasing to God: His own flesh, His own blood:

> "For such an high priest became us, who is holy, harmless, undefiled, separate from sinners, and made higher than the heavens; Who needeth not daily, as those high priests, to offer up sacrifice, first for his own sins, and then for the people's: for this he did once, when he offered up himself. For the law maketh men high priests which have infirmity; but the word of the oath, which was since the law, maketh the Son, who is consecrated for evermore."[109]

---

* Hebrews 10:11
[109] Hebrews 7:26-28

There is no need to explain. The Word again speaks for itself. Christ offered up a Sacrifice to God, once and for all. He was and is the only truly worthy High Priest.

Ever.

And in all my research and study of the Bible, I have been unable to find any passage of Scripture anywhere that states that someone else may go before the Father to offer a redemptive sacrifice on my behalf. Not Moses, nor any of the prophets, nor any of the apostles, nor any of the disciples. Only Jesus.

I say this to set the stage again for what you are about to read. What follows is a catalog of messages which have been quoted from apparitions of Mary and apparitions of St. Michael the Archangel around the world and throughout history. They portray a benevolent representative, who is humbly placing sacrifices before God and Jesus Christ, over and over again on behalf of sinful man in reparation for the sin of the world. They portray a loving, caring high priestess who goes before God to offer a redemptive sacrifice on our behalf: Mary.

Apparition of Mary to the children of Medjugorje, Bosnia 1981-present

> "I am with you and day after day I offer your sacrifices and prayers to God for the salvation of the world."[110]

Interior Locution of Mary to Cyndi Cain, Bella Vista, Arkansas 1989-present

> "Ask the heavenly Father to permit my Immaculate Heart to Triumph. Pray. Be my little victims, for so many souls are saved by your loving sacrifice."[111]

---

[110] *Caritas of Birmingham*, "Messages From Our Lady," September-December 1990 issue, pg. 1. Message of November 25, 1990

[111] *A Call to Peace*, vol. 4, no. 1, "1992 Locutions from the Hidden Flower of the Immaculate Heart," pg. 15. Message of August 14, 1992

Apparition of Mary to Nancy Fowler, Conyers, Georgia, USA
1987-present

"Dear children, thank you for responding to my call here in Conyers. I call all my children here. Thank you for your prayers and sacrifices. My Son receives all your prayers and sacrifices and He stopped the war."[112]

"I cannot restrain my Son's hand. Please help me help you. Offer your daily sacrifices and prayers, please, in reparation for the sins of the world."[113]

Interior Locution of Mary to Father Don Stephano Gobbi, Italy
1973-present

"Live in prayer. Live in trust. Live in the precious hour of your priestly immolation with me, your tender Mother, who has received you all into the garden of her Immaculate Heart, to offer you to the Heavenly Father as victims, pleasing to Him, for the salvation of the world."[114]

Apparition of St. Michael the Archangel to Lucia Abóbora, Fátima, Portugal
1916

"Most Holy Trinity, Father, Son, Holy Spirit, I adore You profoundly and offer You the most precious Body, Blood, Soul and Divinity of Jesus Christ, present in all the tabernacles of the earth, in reparation for the outrages, sacrileges, and indifference with which He Himself is offended. And through the infinite merits of His Most Sacred Heart and of the

---

[112] *To Bear Witness*, pg. 75, para. 106. Message of March 13, 1991. The reference is to the Gulf War of 1991.

[113] The Apparition of Mary's message to the United States, October 13, 1992

[114] *Our Lady Queen of Peace*, "Interior Locutions," pg. 6. Message of November 12, 1988. Used by permission

Immaculate Heart of Mary, I beg of You the conversion of poor sinners."[115]

Apparition of Mary to Theresa Lopez, Denver, Colorado, USA
1991-present

"I am with you day after day; I offer your prayers and sacrifices to God for the salvation of the world."[116]

"God has placed His complete trust in me. I particularly protect those who have been consecrated to me. I cannot help those who do not pray or do no sacrifice."[117]

Apparition of Mary to Lucia Abóbora, Fátima, Portugal
1917

"Do you wish to offer yourselves to God, to endure all the suffering that He may please to send you, as an act of reparation for the sins by which He is offended, and to ask for the conversion of sinners? ...Pray, pray a great deal, and make sacrifices for sinners, for many souls go to hell because they have no one to sacrifice and pray for them."[118]

Apparition of Mary to Sister Agnes Sasagawa, Akita, Japan
1973-1981

"With my Son I have intervened so many times to appease the wrath of the Father. I have prevented the coming of calamities by offering Him the sufferings of the Son on the Cross, His Precious Blood, and beloved souls who console Him forming a cohort of victim

---

115 Walsh, *Our Lady of Fátima*, pp. 41-2
116 Kuntz, pg. 61. Message from November 4, 1991
117 Kuntz, pg. 54. Message from July 28, 1991
118 Walsh, *Our Lady of Fátima*, pp. 51-2, 120

souls. Prayer, penance and courageous sacrifices can
soften the Father's anger."[119]

Apparition of Mary to Sister Mary of Agreda, Spain circa 1617

"Then She offered to the eternal Father the blood,
which his Son shed in the Circumcision and his
humility in allowing Himself to be circumcised in his
sinlessness."[120]

There are many more references, but the point is clear. Only
One Person is worthy of offering any sacrifices, only one Offering
is necessary, only one Offering is pleasing to the Father, and It
has already been given. Nothing can be added to It or taken away,
and the only One who could offer the Sacrifice once and for all
has already done so. The issue is not one of a need for someone to
offer sacrifices before God—rather it is an issue of Whom it is
that actually can. The issue is not one of a lack of sacrifices, but
rather a lack of faith in the One Sacrifice God made as a punishment for sin. We needed Someone to pay the complete price for
our sin and to offer a Sacrifice before the Father to pay for our
rebellion.

Only Jesus can.

Only Jesus did.

The apparition of Mary and its cohorts are not at all who they
claim to be. They are teaching a false gospel.

---

[119] *Our Lady Queen of Peace*, "Church Approves Messages, Weeping
Statue as Supernatural," pg. 16. Message of August 3, 1973. Used by
permission
[120] Mary of Agreda, *Mystical City of God*, Volume IV, *The Coronation*,
pg. 565, para. 666

Messiah

Neither is there salvation in any other: for there is
none other name under heaven given among men,
whereby we must be saved.
—Acts 4:12

FROM the first day Adam looked up and realized that he
was separated from God, humanity has had some sense of
a divine figure who obligates us to obey a moral law and
who punishes our disobedience to it. For any who have
ever tried to bind themselves to obedience to any law—either the
Law of Moses as the Jews have, or to some new kind of "New
Testament Law," as some today have done—it always has the
same result: utter failure. And, as James points out and our own
failures make clear, failure on one point really means to fail the
whole law.* If we are honest with ourselves here, it becomes clear
that our failure to obey demonstrates our complete inability to
save ourselves. We need someone who can rescue us from our
own depravity. We need Someone Who can save us.

And in spite of man's efforts to save himself, which basically
really is rebellion, and in spite of our utter filthiness in comparison to Him, God has in Christ reconciled sinners to Himself:

> "But God commendeth his love toward us, in that,
> while we were yet sinners, Christ died for us."[121]

And in doing so, Christ proved Himself to be the Savior of
the world. God, in order to satisfy His righteous anger, punished

---

* James 2:10
[121] Romans 5:8

His Son in the place of sinners who really deserved it. It is exactly this to which the Jews were blinded, and in rejecting Christ they rejected the only One Who could fulfill the law in their place. And today, just as the Jews did, people often reject God by seeking to be saved on their own, and by their own obedience to a law.

But Christ came into the world knowing that the whole world was already condemned in Adam for Adam's disobedience, and that no law could save them. He knew that He did not need to condemn the world. He needed to save it:

> "For God sent not his Son into the world to condemn
> the world; but that the world through him might be
> saved."[122]

God's clear purpose is this: to honor the agreement He made with Christ before the foundation of the world by giving to Christ those whom He had promised. And Christ received those whom the Father had given, obeying the Law for them on their behalf.*

And in all my research, I have been unable to find anyone ever in all of human history who has met all of these requirements of the Messiah except Jesus. Not Moses, nor any of the prophets, nor any of the apostles, nor any of the disciples. Nobody in the history of mankind has ever fulfilled every single Messianic prophecy and every single point of the Law like Jesus did. He is the only one. He is the Messiah, the Son of the Living God. He came to save us.

I say this to set the stage again for what you are about to read. What follows is a catalog of messages which have been quoted from apparitions of Mary and apparitions of Jesus around the world and throughout history. They portray a kind, loving savior who wishes only to reconcile sinful people to their God. They portray a magnificent, selfless and giving savior who can crush the head of Satan, who can wash our sins away and finally set us free: Mary.

Apparition of Mary to Julia Kim, Naju, South Korea 1985-present

> "The world goes relentlessly to its ruin while Satan
> deploys all his power to destroy it. I wish to save the

---

[122] John 3:17
* John 17:4-6

world by the victory of my mercy and love. That is why my Immaculate Heart will triumph."[123]

Apparition of Mary to the children of Medjugorje, Bosnia 1981-present

"I beg you to give yourselves to me so that I can offer you clean and without sin as a gift to God."[124]

"I seek your prayers, that you may offer them to me for those who are under Satan's influence, that they may be saved."[125]

"I love you with my motherly love and I call upon you to open yourselves completely to me, so that through each of you I may be enabled to convert and save the world, where there is much sin and many things that are evil."[126]

Apparition of Mary to Theresa Lopez, Denver, Colorado, USA
1991-present

"I have come to save the world through you, dear children."[127]

Apparition of Mary to Estela Ruiz, Phoenix, Arizona, USA 1988-present

"Satan has claimed many souls. Know that I am here in the world to defeat him."[128]

---

[123] "Marian Apparitions of the 20th Century: A Message of Urgency"

[124] O'Carroll, pg. 171. Message of August 1, 1985. See Jude 24-5

[125] O'Carroll, pg. 222. Message of February 25, 1988

[126] *Caritas of Birmingham*, June-October 1992 edition, pp. 1-2. Message of August 25, 1992

[127] Kuntz, pp. 61-2. Message of November 10, 1991

[128] *Our Lady Queen of Peace*, "Messages from Our Lady of the Americas," pg. 9. Message of January 13, 1991. Used by permission

Apparition of Mary to Alan de la Roche, Holland 1463

"...immense volumes would have to be written if all
the miracles of my Holy Rosary were to be recorded...
The Rosary shall be the most powerful armor against
hell; it shall destroy vices, weaken sin, overthrow
unbelief ...it shall obtain for souls abundant mercies of
God ...Oh, how many souls will be sanctified by this
means! ...The soul which has recourse to me through
the Rosary shall not perish. ...Every day I deliver from
purgatory souls devoted to my Rosary."[129]

Apparition of Mary to Sister Agnes Sasagawa, Akita, Japan 1973-1981

"I alone am able still to save you from the calamities
which approach. Those who place their confidence in
me will be saved."[130]

Apparition of Mary to Mafalda Mattia, Oliveto Citra, Italy 1985

"I will engage in the final struggle against Satan which
will conclude with the triumph of my Immaculate
Heart and with the coming of the kingdom of God in
the world."[131]

Apparition of Mary to St. Simon Stock, Cambridge, England 1251

"This shall be to you and all Carmelites a privilege,
that anyone who dies clothed in this shall not suffer
eternal fire; and if wearing it they die, they shall be

[129] Ball, pp. 119-20

[130] *Our Lady Queen of Peace*, "Church Approves Messages, Weeping
Statue as Supernatural," pg. 16. Message of October 13, 1973. Used by
permission

[131] *Our Lady Queen of Peace,* "Our Lady in Italy," pg. 14. Message of
January 10, 1986. Used by permission

saved." (Reference is to the Brown Scapular of Our Lady of Mt. Carmel)[132]

Apparition of Mary to Renato Baron, Oliveto Citra, Italy 1985

"I appear in all parts of the world, to change the world, to take away the sin through which men are preparing the destruction of the world."[133]

Apparition of Mary to Marina Kizyn, Hrushiv, Ukraine, Former USSR 1987

"Remember that the Rosary will preserve mankind from sin and perdition."[134]

Apparition of Jesus to Gladys Quiroga de Motta, San Nicolás, Argentina 1983-1989

"In the past, the world was saved by the Ark of Noah. Today my mother is the Ark. It is through her, that souls will be saved, because she will lead them to me. He who rejects my mother, rejects me."[135]

Apparition of Jesus to Nancy Fowler, Conyers, Georgia, USA 1987-present

"I am Jesus, Son of the Living God. I was born of My Holy Mother, Blessed Virgin Mary, who will crush the head of Satan."[136]

---

[132] Cruz, pp. 26-7

[133] *Our Lady Queen of Peace*, "Jesus to the World: My Mother Must be Heard in the Totality of Her Messages," pg. 18. Message from 1985. Used by permission

[134] *Our Lady Queen of Peace*, "Our Lady in Hrushiv," pg. 15. Message of April 27, 1987. Used by permission

[135] *Our Lady Queen of Peace*, "An Urgent Appeal: Our Lady in Argentina," pg. 7. Message of December 30, 1989. Used by permission

[136] *To Bear Witness*, pg. 58, para. 65. Message of November 17, 1990

Apparition of Mary to Juan Angel Collado, Sabana Grande, Puerto Rico
1953

> "I promise to facilitate and/or provide the necessary graces for salvation before death to all those who, in times of confusion and of definition of the way towards my most Beloved Son, promulgate my name as Mother of the True Way to the Father."[137]

These are only a few of the quotes I have been able to locate. There are many more, but the issue is not one of a need for a Savior—rather it is an issue of Whom it is that actually has the power to save. We need someone who can wash away our sins and make our souls as white as snow. We need someone who can present us unblemished before the throne of God. We need someone to save us from the wrath we rightfully deserve.

Only Jesus can.

Only Jesus does.

The apparition of Mary and its cohorts are not at all who they claim to be. They are teaching a false gospel.

---

[137] *Our Lady Queen of Peace*, "Our Lady of the Rosary in Puerto Rico," pg. 13. Message of April 23, 1953. Used by permission. This is a little confusing, but simply put, the message here is, "I will save whoever preaches my name to anyone who is not sure how to get into Heaven."

Goddess

In the beginning was the Word,
and the Word was with God,
and the Word was God.
—John 1:1

IT has often been said that Religion is defined as man seeking God, while Christianity is God seeking man. And so it is. Religion is a set of rules that people set up, obedience to which determines one's access to Heaven. Christianity, on the other hand, is a set of rules set up by God, obedience to which also determines one's access to Heaven. The difference? Well, according to Religion, the rules indicate that some people *actually deserve to make it to Heaven*. There is an implied but definite cut-off point, after which nobody can get in, which means there is a definite number who can make it in just by obeying the rules.

But according to Christianity, *nobody* can make it. The rules are established by God Himself, and if you fail on one point of the rules, you have failed the whole test.* This may seem unfair to some, but God makes the rules, and by His rules all are denied access, because in Adam, all failed.

But the same God Who made the rules of Christianity, Who declared that only perfect people can get into Heaven,† also has a plan to bring his children home to Himself in Christ:

> "...thou hast given him power over all flesh, that he should give eternal life to as many as thou hast given him"[138]

---

* James 2:10
† Matthew 5:48
[138] John 17:2

Because He loved the world so much, He purposed to seek out His lost children, to search them out one by one and rescue them. And He spared no expense in doing so.

He Who made the rules would ultimately be the only One to abide by them. If only perfect people can get into Heaven, then only perfect people would go. And only perfect people can.

God provided a way by which His children could be declared perfect. To do this, He caused His Son to bear our imperfections, so that while our shortcomings and faults were all placed on the shoulders of Jesus Christ, the perfection of the Son was conferred on those who believe.

So the rules still apply. Only perfect people can go to Heaven. Because God loves His own so much, He spanned the greatest distance to show the greatest love, to rescue the greatest sinners, and He died the most humiliating death to do it. To declare His children righteous. To bring them home.

This is the Gospel. It is simple. It is straightforward. It is true.

It is also impossible. So impossible, that it took God to accomplish it as only He can. And there is only one Gospel. And only one God. There is no other.

And no matter where I search in the Scriptures, I cannot find anything at all that suggests that I worship, praise and adore anyone else but Yahweh, the God of Israel. Not Moses, nor any of the prophets, nor any of the apostles, nor any of the disciples. No one but God, Himself.

Why do I make this point? Because only God could do what He did. I emphasize this point especially since what you are about to read may offend you the most. What follows is a catalog of messages which have been quoted from apparitions of Mary and apparitions of Jesus around the world and throughout history. They portray an all-powerful, omnipresent, everlasting goddess who wants to save you, who is worthy of being glorified, and who will ultimately judge how well you obeyed the rules. They portray a majestic monarch who sits at the right hand of God, and for whom the seventh day of the week is reserved as holy. They portray the bright morning star who shares the divinity of the Father, the Son and the Holy Spirit, and who has the infinite power to transcend the unfathomable distance between a Righteous God and sinful man. They portray a goddess who rules Heaven and Earth and everything under the Earth: Mary.

Apparition of Jesus to Nancy Fowler, Conyers, Georgia, USA 1987-present

> "Look at the four points on the cross. I will explain. See the Holy Trinity of God in three points. See in the other point My Mother, part of the Holy Trinity of God."[139]

> "One branch was selected from all branches. This branch is the most pure, the most delicate, the most perfect of all branches. My Mother is above all creatures and She is elevated to the Throne of God."[140]

Apparition of Mary to the children of Medjugorje, Bosnia 1981-present

> "Dear children, I am giving the graces first of all to the parishioners and then to the others. You must receive the messages first, then the others. You will be answerable to me and to my Son Jesus."[141]

> "Continually adore the Most-holy Sacrament (the Eucharist). I am always present when the faithful are in adoration."[142]

> "I ask you once more to pray especially for my intentions. If you pray for my intentions I will be glorified through you."[143]

> "God sent me to you so that I can help you. If you wish to, grasp for the Rosary. Already, the Rosary alone can do miracles in the world and in your lives."[144]

---

[139] *To Bear Witness*, pg. 38, para. 22. Message of August 14-15, 1990

[140] *To Bear Witness*, pg. 38, para. 22. Message of July 11, 1991

[141] O'Carroll, pg. 176. Message of February 6, 1986

[142] O'Carroll, pg. 160. Message of March 15, 1984. Parentheses added

[143] O'Carroll, pg. 259. Message of November 26, 1988

[144] *Words From Heaven: Messages of Our Lady from Medjugorje*, 5th ed., (Birmingham, AL: Saint James Publishing Company, ©1991) pg.

continued on next page

Interior Locution of Mary to Carlos Lopez, San Francisco, California, USA
1991-present

> "Trust also in your Mother. I am the Morning Star whom announces the day, the Light which is near, the Light of God, the Light of Love, the Light of peace, the Light of eternal salvation... I will ascend to heaven to take possession of My throne alongside of My Son."[145]

Interior Locution of Jesus to Julia Kim, Naju, South Korea
1985-present

> "Tell everyone that accepting My Mother's words is the same as accepting Me and that holding Her hands and following Her is the shortcut to Me."[146]

Apparition of Mary to Sister Mary of Agreda, Spain
circa 1617

> "After placing the most blessed Mary on this exalted and supereminent throne, the Lord declared to the courtiers of heaven all the privileges She should enjoy in virtue of this participation in his majesty. ...At the same time a voice sounded from the throne saying: 'My Beloved, chosen among the creatures, our kingdom is Thine... We give Thee power majesty and sovereignty. Being filled with grace beyond all the rest Thou hast humiliated Thyself in thy own estimation to

---

218. Message of January 25, 1991. The authors wished to be known only as, "Two friends of Medjugorje." In the context of the message to the children of Medjugorje, I believe this was meant to say that "the Rosary by itself," rather than "the Rosary and nothing else" can do miracles in the world.

[145] *Signs of the Times*, Volume 6, Number 2, April/May/June 1994. Published by Signs of the Times, Sterling, Virginia, Maureen Flynn, editor. "Heaven's Global Tapestry," pg. 49. Message of February 2, 1994

[146] *Signs of the Times*, Volume 6, Number 2, April/May/June 1994. "Heaven's Global Tapestry," pg. 46. Message of May 16, 1991

the lowest place; receive now the supreme dignity deserved by Thee and, as a participation in our Divinity, the dominion over all the creatures of our Omnipotence.'*"147

Interior Locution of Mary to Cyndi Cain, Bella Vista, Arkansas
1989-present

"Those who refuse to acknowledge me as Queen of Heaven and Earth will see the might of God and their pride and stubbornness shall bend, their eyes shall perceive Truth and know God is not diminished by bestowing honor upon a mere creature, but rather, is exalted because of my virtue and obedience."148

Interior Locution of Jesus to Cyndi Cain, Bella Vista, Arkansas
1989-present

"My little ones, I ask you to listen to the words of My Mother, for they are My Words and My Infinite Graces and Merits which She, the Eternal Virgin, dispenses. Yes, Eternal, for before time began She was known to the Trinity."149

Apparition of Mary to Maximin Giraud and Melanie Mathieu, LaSalette, France
1846

"I gave you six days for working. The seventh I have reserved for myself. But no one will give it to me. This

---

* I realize this is a little rich, but it was actually prescribed reading for Nancy Fowler by the Apparition of Mary at Conyers, Georgia, U.S.A. (See *To Bear Witness*, pp. 65, 123)

147 Mary of Agreda, *Mystical City of God*, Volume IV, *The Coronation*, pp. 655-656, para. 777-8

148 *A Call to Peace*, Volume 4, Number 1, "1992 Locutions from the Hidden Flower of the Immaculate Heart," pg. 3. Message of January 8, 1992. Compare against Philippians 2:6-11

149 *A Call to Peace*, vol. 4, no. 1, "1992 Locutions from the Hidden Flower of the Immaculate Heart," pg. 4. Message of January 23, 1992

is what causes the weight of my Son's arm to be so crushing."[150]

These are only a few of many quotes I have been able to locate. There are more, but I believe these are sufficient to make the point. The issue is not one of the existence of a god, but of Who that God actually is. It is not an issue of whether or not we need someone of infinite power to rescue us. It is rather an issue of Whom it is that has the infinite power to do it—enough power to transcend eternity. It is not an issue of whether we should keep the Sabbath holy, but an issue of Whom we keep it holy for.

But most of all, it is an issue of having a God Who is powerful enough to come down from Heaven to set us free. Only God can do that.

Only Jesus can.

Only Jesus did.

The apparition of Mary and its cohorts are not at all who they claim to be. They are teaching a false gospel.

---

[150] Lord, pg. 70. Message of September 19, 1846

Part III Solo Christo

Who hath ascended up into heaven, or descended? who hath gathered the wind in his fists? who hath bound the waters in a garment? who hath established all the ends of the earth? what is his name, and what is his son's name, if thou canst tell?

—*Proverbs 30:4*

By Their Fruits...

> Let no man beguile you of your reward in a
> voluntary humility and worshipping of angels,
> intruding into those things which he hath not seen,
> vainly puffed up by his fleshly mind.
> —*Colossians 2:18*

ALMOST without exception proponents of the apparitions of Mary will contest my findings and reject my urgent plea that the apparitions be tested. They respond with the statement, "But we *do* test the apparitions of Mary—by their fruits!" The basis for this position, of course, is the Gospel of Matthew, wherein Christ warned His followers to be on guard against false prophets "which come to you in sheep's clothing, but inwardly they are ravening wolves."[151] Christ's warning here is accompanied by the test with which false prophets should be discerned: "Ye shall know them by their fruits."[152] And I do not disagree.

But it can be clearly seen in the verses that follow that Jesus was not prescribing a test of spirits, but of *people* who falsely claim to be Christians. In verses 21 through 23 of that chapter He describes the pitiful pleas of *actual humans* who, though they performed a wealth of good works during their earthly lives, are still denied entrance into Heaven on the Day of Judgment. Why? Because they were trusting in their own righteousness to gain entrance instead of trusting solely in Christ's completed work on the cross. It is at this point that we see the error in using this passage as a test of spirits. It clearly is not. These wolves in

---

[151] Matthew 7:15b

[152] Matthew 7:16a

sheep's clothing who beg to be let into Heaven are not demonic spirits or unholy angels. They are humans who never entered into a personal relationship with Jesus Christ, for He rebukes them, saying, "I never knew you: depart from me."[153]

But the insistence of apparition proponents that this passage be used as a test of spirits provides a unique opportunity to assess their fruits without risking the appearance of self-righteous judgment. For while the passage in Matthew 7 does not provide a test of spirits, it does indicate that the fruits of those who claim to be Christians should be in accordance with the Gospel of Jesus Christ. Unfortunately, the fruits of the apparitions fail this test as well. And though it is true that the apparitions almost always result in prayer, fasting and 'conversion,' we cannot overlook the fact that fruits are not to be considered an end in themselves. This mistake was made by Ivan Dugandzic, a Franciscan friar in Medjugorje, when he contested the findings of the committee investigating the origin of the apparitions there.

In 1983, when the committee returned a judgment which determined that the apparitions were not of divine origin,* Ivan Dugandzic wrote to the bishop to voice his disagreement. Appealing to the good fruits of the apparitions, Dugandzic wrote,

> "Is it possible that Satan can be divided against himself and not fall? Has he come to the conclusion that his usual schemes to bring man to damnation are not working so that he has to fall back on the extreme resorts of prayer and fasting?"[154]

Indeed, such an appeal to good fruits cannot go unanswered, but we must not appeal to fruits based solely on their own merit. Rather, any fruits that result from the sightings of Mary should be consistent with the Gospel of Jesus Christ. Some followers of the apparitions of Mary provide tacit acknowledgment of this principle, albeit in a different context, when they write,

---

[153] Matthew 7:23

* This judgment is not considered final, and pilgrimages to Medjugorje, accompanied by devotion to that apparition, are still considered acceptable until a final determination is made.

[154] O'Carroll, pg. 244. From Ivan Dugandzic's letter to Pavao Zanic, Bishop of Mostar, dated September 22, 1987

> "There are some apparitions that awaken the faith and which are granted by God, but an increasing number of 'alleged' apparitions and inner locutions which claim to be guiding the world and offer a plan to save mankind cannot be accepted. Just because the messages are similar or one *feels* good when visiting the site where an alleged apparition or inner locution is taking place does not make it valid."[155]

Their point is well made—fruits in and of themselves are necessary but are not sufficient as a determining factor. On this point, we all can agree. We know that many false religions in the world instruct people to pray and fast. But for what purpose? These are undoubtedly 'fruits' of some sort, but they are hardly consistent with the Gospel. And of what merit is 'conversion' if it is not conversion to Christ? Conversion to Mary or the Blessed Mother is not a fruit that should result from the preaching of the Gospel, and neither does the Bible request it. But it is just such fruit as this that we see coming from the apparitions of Mary. Similarly, prayers directed to Mary and the other saints are not consistent with the teaching of the Gospel, but the apparitions of Mary instruct people to pray in exactly that way.*

So exactly which fruits *do* validate an apparition? No guidelines have been suggested by those who insist that we test them by that means, but Jesus provides the only guidelines we need. His test of human false prophets in Matthew 7 has its basis in the Gospel that Paul would one day echo by writing that God saved us,

> "Not by works of righteousness which we have done, but according to his mercy..."[156]

It is by this same Gospel that we may assess the fruits of the apparitions. And we discover that in spite of all the prayer and

---

[155] *Caritas of Birmingham*, May-August 1991 edition, pg. 10. Emphasis in original

* Proponents of the apparitions contend that they do not pray *to* the saints, but rather ask them to pray for us. Such prayers as "the Hail Holy Queen" and the "Prayer to St. Michael" disprove this notion, as they begin, "Hail Holy queen...to thee do we cry," and "St. Michael, defend us in battle; be our protection..."(de Montfort, pg. 1)

[156] Titus 3:5a

fasting, the followers of the apparitions have found themselves trusting in their own works, or those of Mary, rather than trusting in the cleansing blood of Jesus Christ to save them. And we see that their 'conversions' are not consistent with what the Bible teaches on the matter. They have fallen into the same trap as those who were crying out in Matthew 7:22, "Lord, Lord, have we not prophesied in thy name? and in thy name have cast out devils? and in thy name done many wonderful works?" The cries of the apparitionists on that Day may be just as futile: 'Did we not pray the Rosary? Did we not offer sacrifices to Your mother in reparation for the sins of the world? Did we not place our trust in Mary? Did we not pray, fast and convert to the blessed mother?'

Though it may seem to be an incredible presumption to suggest that such things have entered the minds of the apparition's followers, their testimonies are full of similar statements. Pilgrims have traveled to the ends of the earth to see apparitions, experience the peace those apparitions seem to bring, and find the answer to one simple question: "How does one gain entrance into Heaven?" The apparitions of Mary have yet to give them the proper answer. Consider the following nine testimonies of those who follow them. They portray a sincerity and devotion that is beyond question, but they also reveal a gospel which is not.

1) Nancy Fowler, the visionary who receives messages and visions from the apparition of Mary in Conyers, Georgia was allowed to see glimpses of Heaven and hell during several of her many apparitions. Yet she still does not know that salvation is a free gift—something which she cannot obtain by good works:

> "Nancy says that her experiences of hell are enough to make one work, to do everything, and to speak the truth to help everyone escape this fate. On the other hand, her visits to Heaven were such that she finds difficulty in describing what it was like. 'It was so profound, so beautiful, so peaceful, that it is worth working all one's life to get there.'"[157]

I don't doubt Nancy's sincerity, but I question her theology. If she plans on working her whole life to get to Heaven, the Bible assures us that she will not make it there—because Heaven is not

---

[157] *To Bear Witness*, pg. 4

for sale and our works cannot gain entrance for us. The teachings of the apparitions of Mary are yielding bad fruits of the very nature that Christ warned us about in Matthew 7:21-23.

2) Anna Graham, after returning from Medjugorje, published a booklet entitled, *Diary of a Pilgrim to Medjugorje*, in which she wrote about her experiences there. On one occasion, a priest taught her about God's relationship with Adam and Eve, and about the results of the fall of mankind. The priest's homily emphasized 'the role of Mary in our salvation and in the work of the Church,' and Anna relates what the priest taught her about it:

> "At that moment when God spoke to them of their disobeying deed he promised them they would be saved. It was then God planned a woman, Mary, to reconcile man with his God. Mary then becomes the first savior at her birth... a special creature... the Immaculate Conception."[158]

But the Scriptures tell us that it was Christ, not Mary, who reconciled man to God by making peace between us through the blood of the cross.[*] So if Anna has placed her trust in Mary as 'the first savior,' the Bible again assures us that she will not gain entrance into Heaven, for there is one Name and one Name only by which we must be saved.[†] The teachings of the apparitions of Mary contradict this and are yielding bad fruits by instructing people to trust in Mary as their personal savior.

3) When John Radzilowicz, a Catholic deacon, witnessed his wife's healing at Medjugorje, he became a devout follower of Mary. Because of this miracle (a healing which I do not dispute), he now claims Mary as the primary intercessor:

> "Well, first of all, I have no authority to speak for the Catholic Church, but I'm speaking from my heart... Well, the main difference between other Christians and us is that we revere the Blessed Mother, the

---

[158] Graham, Anna, *Diary of a Pilgrim to Medjugorje*, December 4, 1988, pp. 3-4. Ellipses in original

[*] Colossians 1:20

[†] Acts 4:12

Catholics do. Now, Jesus and God are the boss, but
Mary is the greatest intercessor..."[159]

But the Scriptures tell us that Jesus is the greatest intercessor, and
it is Jesus, not Mary, Who "ever liveth to make intercession" for
us.[160] If John is planning on gaining entrance into Heaven by the
intercession of Mary, the Bible assures us that he will not make it
there, for there is only one mediator between God and man.[*] The
teachings of the apparitions of Mary contradict this and are
yielding bad fruits which cause people to trust in Mary—even
above Jesus Christ—to intercede for them before God.

4) A recent issue of *The Mir Response*, a magazine dedicated to
the distribution of the Medjugorje messages, featured an article
about Steve Drennan, a young man who had recently experienced
a dramatic conversion in his life. His testimony appeared under
the title, "'I Want to Be a Saint!' A Teen Gives His Life To
Christ." He wrote, "Now, at 19, I want to give my life to God
through Our Lady."[161] But if Steve has given his life to God
through Mary he can be assured that God has not received it, for
Mary is not the means by which we gain access to the Father.
Jesus is, and *only* Jesus.[†] The teachings of the apparitions of Mary
contradict this and are yielding bad fruits which cause people to
believe they can enter into a personal relationship with God
through Mary.

5) During the Marian Medjugorje Conference that took place in
New Orleans, Louisiana in December of 1991, a woman named
Lylan Mitchell testified that she had been a Buddhist her whole
life, and finally "converted to the Blessed Mother"[162] after a

---

[159] *Geraldo*, Host: Geraldo Rivera, air date December 20, 1991 under
the title, "Do You Believe in Miracles?" transcript #1112, pg. 14. ©1991
by the Investigative News Group, Inc. Transcr. by Journal Graphics, Inc.
[160] Hebrews 7:25b
[*] 1 Timothy 2:5
[161] *The Mir Response*, Volume 4, Number 6, December 1992/January
1993 issue, "I Want to Be a Saint!: A Teen Gives His Life to Christ," pp.
39,40
[†] John 14:6
[162] From a video recording of the 1991 Marian Medjugorje Conference
in New Orleans, LA, USA, "The Testimony of Lylan Mitchell"

pilgrimage to Medjugorje, where she experienced an actual physical healing. This woman later died of another illness, receiving messages from the apparitions of Jesus and Mary up to the moment of her death. She received these messages through the interior locutions of a close friend, and the last message she received from the apparition of Jesus was,

> "My beloved Lylan, I am Jesus who loves you... Your suffering has made atonement for many, many, many souls... When you come to me, I will show you many, many souls that you have saved."[163]

But conversion to Mary is not mentioned anywhere in the Bible as a means of salvation. And nowhere does Scripture teach that I can make atonement for anyone at all through my own sufferings. There is only one Name under Heaven by which we can be saved: Jesus Christ.* It is by His payment alone that any soul can be redeemed and be reconciled to the Father. Lylan died without ever hearing that from the apparitions. The teachings of the apparitions are yielding such bad fruits as these, and are causing people to trust in their own suffering rather than that of Jesus Christ in order to gain eternal life.

6) In Medjugorje, several pilgrims were asked what they would want to know from the apparition of Mary if an audience was granted. One pilgrim stated that she would ask:

> "Am I worthy? How do you know when you're living your life right, and how do you know that you're worthy to go to Heaven?"[164]

If this woman really wants to know if she is living her life right and if she is worthy of going to Heaven, the Bible has a simple answer: You're not. And neither am I. I am not living my life, nor is that pilgrim living hers, in a manner that is worthy of gaining eternal life. Scripture states clearly that I cannot, for I have sinned

---

[163] *The Mir Response,* Volume 5, Number 2, April/May 1993 issue, "You Are My Chosen Victim: Christ Called Lylan Mitchell to Help Carry His Cross," pp. 12-13 and 19

* Acts 4:11,12

[164] "Medjugorje: The Lasting Sign"

and fallen short of God's glory.* But I will gain entrance into Heaven anyway. Why? Because even though I could never be good enough to get into Heaven, I have placed my fullest confidence in Someone who is not only worthy of Heaven, but also paid a high enough price to make me worthy, too. The apparitions of Mary are not revealing this simple truth to their followers and are yielding the fruits of self-justification that Christ warned us about in Matthew 7:21-23.

7) A Catholic priest by the name of Harold Cohen has become a follower of the apparitions of Mary, and is a regular teacher on the Eternal Word Television Network which broadcasts from Birmingham, Alabama, USA. His devotion to Mary is quite strong and he frequently refers to her in his teachings. In an article entitled, "Mother of Mercy" which appeared recently in *The Mir Response*, he writes:

> "There's a little story I love to tell. Jesus was walking through Heaven one day, and He saw a lot of people who did not belong there. So He went to Peter and said, 'Peter, what are you doing letting all of these people in?' And Peter answered, 'Lord, I keep telling them to go away, but your Mother keeps letting them in the back door.'"[165]

Cohen qualifies the statement by saying, "The reality behind the story is not that Mary is more merciful than Jesus, but that Mary is a beautiful, feminine reflection of the infinite tenderness of God."[166] But Cohen's efforts to play down the profound theological implications of this story are lost when he quotes from the writings of St. John Chrysostom to further his point:

> "She was chosen from all eternity to be the Mother of God, that those who could not be saved according to the rigor of Divine Justice might be so with the help of her sweet mercy and powerful intercession."[167]

---

* Romans 3:23

[165] "Mother of Mercy," by Harold Cohen, *The Mir Response,* Volume 5, Number 2, April/May 1993 issue, pg. 5

[166] *The Mir Response*, Volume 5, Number 2, April/May 1993, pg. 5

[167] *The Mir Response*, Volume 5, Number 2, April/May 1993, pg. 5

Cohen's meaning is clear. He has concluded that what God cannot save by His infinite justice, Mary can save by her great mercy. This teaching goes far beyond what Biblical Christianity would call blasphemy, and it is the fruit of these apparitions of Mary—a fruit that has long since departed from any clear reflection of the Gospel of Jesus Christ. It is in fact the gospel of Mary that the apparition would have its followers teach, and this false gospel is yielding bad fruits which cause people to believe that Mary can save souls who did not place their faith in Jesus Christ.

8) The most disturbing 'fruit' I have seen to date is that of the teaching of St. Louis de Montfort in his work, *The Secret of the Rosary*. Written in the early 1700s, his book has been through 27 printings since it was first translated into English in 1965, with its latest printing in 1992 numbering 4 million copies. De Montfort's work is distributed worldwide in many languages and contains the reflections of a Catholic saint who lived a lifetime of devotion to Mary and the Rosary. Consider the remarkable statement he makes in his book based on the fact that the Rosary contains as many Hail Marys as there are Psalms in the Bible:

> "Since simple and uneducated people are not able to say the Psalms of David the Rosary is held to be just as fruitful for them as David's Psalter is for others. But the Rosary can be considered even more valuable than the latter for three reasons: Firstly, because the Angelic Psalter [the Rosary] bears a nobler fruit, that of the Word Incarnate, whereas David's Psalter only prophesies His coming; Secondly, just as the real thing is more important than its prefiguration and as the body is more than its shadow, in the same way the Psalter of Our Lady is greater than David's Psalter which did no more than prefigure it; And thirdly, because Our Lady's Psalter (or the Rosary made up of the Our Father and the Hail Mary) is the direct work of the Most Blessed Trinity and was not made through a human instrument."[168]

[168] de Montfort, St. Louis, *The Secret of the Rosary*, (NY: Montfort Publications, ©1965-92) pg. 25, trans. Mary Barbour, T.O.P. Brackets added for clarity, parentheses in original

Although the followers of the apparitions have emphatically claimed that the apparitions' teachings are not greater than God's Word (see above, pg. 51), we have here possibly the greatest proponent of the Rosary and the apparitions, a canonized saint of the Catholic Church, and his writings indicate quite the opposite. De Montfort's teaching is sadly resonant of Christ's parable of the Sower, in which Satan prohibits people from hearing the truth by stealing the Word from their hearts, "lest they should believe and be saved."[169] De Montfort's assertion that the Rosary is greater than the Psalms of David, or that it is more profitable to recite the Rosary than to read the Psalms, amounts to nothing less than the deception portrayed in that parable. The Rosary is the product of these apparitions and is yielding bad fruits which cause people to trust in the Rosary, even above the Word of God, as a means of sanctification.

9) Every year in New Orleans, Louisiana, USA, apparition enthusiasts from all over the world gather for a conference in honor of the most celebrated apparitions occurring today: those of Medjugorje, Bosnia. And every year a song sheet is distributed containing the songs of praise and worship to be sung at that year's conference. The 1991 Marian Medjugorje Conference song sheet included a chorus called "Mother of Peace," which begins with the following stanza:

> "Mother of peace, Mother of love,
> Come see our joy now, praising your words."[170]

What de Montfort began by devaluing God's Word in the Psalms of David, the apparition's followers have completed by elevating its words to the status of Scripture. It was not stated outright in the chorus, but the implication is there. Singing that we are "praising" Mary's words could hardly mean anything else considering that David reserved such sentiments for God's Word alone.* It is most unfortunate after God promised that His Word

---

[169] Luke 8:12b

[170] *The Mir Response*, Volume 3, Number 6, Conference Edition, December 1991, pg. 23. Words to "Mother of Peace" by Michael B. Lynch, ©1976 Raven Music

* Psalms 56:4,10 (Psalms 56:5,11 in the New American Bible)

would be written on our hearts as a sign of the New Covenant,* that these people should be satisfied with having the apparition's words written on theirs. Praising the words of an apparition is a questionable fruit that causes people to trust in something other than God's written revelation to us as a source of Truth.

The apparition's words are not to be praised. They are to be questioned and put to the test—something that its followers are genuinely unwilling, and perhaps even unequipped, to do. This observation may seem inequitable, but the only means by which the Body of Christ can be equipped to test the spirits is to be familiar with the means that God has provided for testing them: His Word. But those who follow the apparitions are often unable to discern between what is God's Word and what is merely the teaching of a vision. Bud Macfarlane, an avid proponent of the apparitions, described as being "one of the top experts, if not *the* top expert, on this subject in the country,"[171] once explained about three days of darkness that have been prophesied by the apparitions. To substantiate their teachings, he referred to the same prophecy in the book of Isaiah and in the New Testament, stating:

> "Many of you have read about the three days of darkness that's been much publicized by mystics for the last two centuries, and a similar supernatural intervention where the earth will be darkened. And you see in the Scriptures as well, in Isaiah, about the moon and the sun not giving their light for a period of three days."[172]

> "The three days of darkness [is] in various prophecies. It's even in the Scripture. It's in the New Testament, it's in Isaiah, relative to this period where the sun will be darkened and the moon won't give it's light."[173]

---

* Jeremiah 31:33

[171] Macfarlane, Bud, Sr., M.I., of the Mary Foundation, in his speech entitled, "Update on Marian Apparitions," on March 25, 1992 at Sacred Heart Catholic Church, Wadsworth, OH. Emphasis in original

[172] Macfarlane, Bud, Sr., M.I., "Update on Marian Apparitions"

[173] From the tape: "The Coming Tribulations," a speech given by Bud Macfarlane, Sr., M.I., to a group of Mary Foundation friends and benefactors on August 7, 1993, Westlake, OH

Perhaps Macfarlane was referring to Isaiah 13:10 and Matthew 24:29, which indeed refer to the sun, moon and stars losing their light, or perhaps to Isaiah 60:2, which prophesies that darkness will cover the earth. But for a period of three days? There is no such prophecy in the entire Bible, much less in the writings of Isaiah.[†] The prophet Isaiah taught nothing of the sort, and Macfarlane has committed the grievous error of confusing the teachings of apparitions for the Word of God. Certainly there is room in God's Kingdom for people who make honest mistakes, but God has shown very little tolerance in the past for people who put words in His mouth.[*] Macfarlane's error is now repeated thousands of times over on audio cassettes distributed by the Mary Foundation to warn people of the urgency of Mary's messages. And though any apparitionist would concede that the teachings of the apparitions are not the Word of God, those who listen to tapes from the Mary Foundation are now hearing them as if they were—a dangerous mistake, to say the least. And to contribute to the utter confusion that the apparitions have brought about, Macfarlane, after clearly asserting that the prophecy of three days of darkness is a scriptural prophecy—which it is not— then told his listeners that the prophecy may not even come true:

> "But again, there's no guarantee that we will ever have
> a period of three days of darkness although there are
> many mystics who make references to it."[174]

By elevating the teachings and rituals of the apparitions above the Bible, and sometimes even confusing them with it, de Montfort and other apparitionists reveal the true nature of their fruits. And though it can be reasonably argued that the Rosary has its basis in Scripture (as the Our Father and the first half of the Hail Mary find their origins there), and that Scriptures prophesy that the sun and moon will one day be darkened, we can safely state that the rituals and instructions of the apparitions defy the teachings of these same Scriptures: that God's Word is exalted above all other things,[°] and that Christians are to avoid useless

---

[†] Exodus 10:22-23 would not qualify, as it was not a prophecy and was limited to the Land of Egypt

[*] See, for example, Deuteronomy 13:1-6 and Jeremiah 28

[174] Macfarlane, Bud, Sr., M.I., "The Coming Tribulations"

[°] Psalms 138:2

repetitions when they pray.§ These rituals and teachings then
become the means by which the followers of the apparitions have
had the Word of God stolen from their hearts. Therefore, they are
not hearing the Gospel of Jesus Christ, and in spite of their
repeated recitation of the Rosary and its associated prayers they
have not heard that salvation is a free gift, something they cannot
work for and do not deserve. Despite their sincere praise of the
apparitions' messages, they have yet to hear that it is only Jesus
Who can save them—and only His Word that can sanctify them.°

By this we can conclude that the apparitions of Mary either
do not know the Gospel, or do not desire that any of their
followers should hear it. I have come to the conclusion that the
latter is true and that the apparitions of Mary are deliberately
withholding the true Gospel from their followers. Their fruits and
teachings could hardly indicate that more clearly.

All of these considerations notwithstanding, the Catholic
Church has instructed the faithful that it is better to follow the
apparitions than not. Accompanying almost every book, magazine
or newsletter that circulates messages from the apparitions of
Mary is a disclaimer to the following effect:

> "Finally, we shall also abide by what Pope Urban VII
> stated in the 1600s: 'In cases which concern private
> revelations, it is better to believe, for if you believe
> and it was proven true, you will be happy that you
> have believed because our Holy Mother Church asked
> it. If you believe and it should be proven false, you
> will receive all blessings as if it had been proven true,
> because you believed it to be true.'"[175]

This teaching is widely disseminated by those who follow the
apparitions, but its basis cannot be found in Scripture. In fact,

---

§ Matthew 6:7

° John 17:17

[175] This standard disclaimer can be found in many pro-apparition
magazines, and while it is true that Urban VII probably only intended
this to apply to Church-approved apparitions, the apparition enthusiasts
apply it universally. Two such periodicals that come to mind are *Signs of
the Times*, a magazine that documents Marian apparitions throughout the
world, and *A Call to Peace*, a newspaper periodical which documents
the interior locutions of the apparitions in Bella Vista, Arkansas

Scripture would have us adopt a much more skeptical stance, and
Paul has told us why: "Now the Spirit speaketh expressly, that in
the latter times some shall depart from the faith, giving heed to
seducing spirits, and doctrines of devils."[176] Yet it is by
Urban VII's teaching that many are misled into practicing the
questionable fruits of the apparitions of Mary without regard for
the possibility of deception. The Denver apparitionists even went
so far as to modify the statement of Urban VII to read, "because
our Mother asked it,"[177] omitting "Holy" and "Church" from the
disclaimer. In doing so they implied a transfer of their spiritual
authority from the pope directly to the apparition itself.

On the basis of exactly such fruits as these, I wholly reject the
apparitions of Mary and their teachings. One acquaintance of
mine countered this rejection by saying, "Judge them as you will,
but I cannot reject the apparitions of Our Lady just because some
people do not respond properly. They have to be judged as a
whole, and not as individual parts." This would perhaps be a valid
observation if the fruits discussed here were due to a mere
misinterpretation of the teachings of the visions, but that is just
not the case. The fruits which have been analyzed in this chapter
result from a very rigid adherence to the apparitions' teachings,
and the errors that result are being propagated by some of the
most notable apparition proponents—even canonized saints.
These questionable fruits are being taught by deacons, priests and
saints as if they were the core of Biblical Christianity. They are
not just someone's poor response to the apparitions. They are the
direct result of applying their teachings.

So the error in dismissing the individual fruits is plainly seen.
When I request that the apparitions be tested according to the
Bible, their followers insist that an inspection of their fruits is
sufficient. But when the fruits are found to be Scripturally
unsound, it is considered unfair to judge them based solely on
some people's poor response to them. This elusive method of
avoiding true discernment not only allows for accepting the
apparitions without a Biblical test, but also makes it rather easy to
accept the clearly errant teaching of Pope Urban VII regarding
private revelation. His teaching quite simply instructs us that it is
practically impossible to be misled by the apparitions. With a

---

[176] 1 Timothy 4:1
[177] Kuntz, pg. 20

guarantee like that, it is easy to understand why there is such a reluctance to test them. According to Urban VII, what we do not know, cannot hurt us.

This, then, dilutes the warnings that Christ gave us in the seventh chapter of Matthew. For if the wolves in sheep's clothing can do us no harm, one has to wonder why Jesus would give us such a stern warning against them. It is clear from His teaching that these wolves, though they have been fruitful all their lives, have sprung from a rotten tree that withheld from them the Gospel of Jesus Christ. So He renders His judgment and we must render ours, for He said, "Either make the tree good, and his fruit good; or else make the tree corrupt, and his fruit corrupt: for the tree is known by his fruit."[178] His command leaves no room for such disclaimers as Urban VII's. The fruits of the apparitions are not consistent with the Gospel of Jesus Christ, and the apparitions comprise the rotten tree from which these fruits spring. They are therefore to be rejected. And though "by their fruits" is not the test of spirits and is never identified as such in the Scriptures, it is certainly a means by which we can discern the fruits of the apparition phenomenon as well as the spiritual condition of those who display them. Perhaps this sounds like self-righteous judgment on my part, but I remind those who would take offense that this judgment has been exercised at the invitation of the apparitions' followers and at the command of Jesus Christ; we have *all* been asked to judge the fruits of apparitions.

But since an examination of their fruits does not lend conclusive support to the claims of the apparitions, a final, hollow defense is offered by their proponents:

> "For one who believes in them, no explanation is necessary. For one who does not believe in them, no explanation is possible."[*]

It is always a disappointment to me when I hear this defense offered, because we are instructed in Scripture to be skeptical of

---

[178] Matthew 12:33

[*] This explanation has been used frequently by the visionaries and by their many followers. An example of its use was demonstrated on the *Geraldo* broadcast of December 20, 1991. See footnote 159 of this chapter

all spirits until they submit to the test. We are told to test *all* teachings using the Word of God, as did the Bereans in Acts 17:11. We are to submit to the Bible in these matters, for it is useful for correcting those who have been misled by false teachings.[†] And above all, we are instructed that we *are* to have an explanation ready for those who question our beliefs.[§] So if the apparitions' followers cannot offer a satisfactory explanation for following a spirit that teaches a false gospel, then their devotion, sincere as it might be, is to be rejected, as are the fruits that result from it.

A friend of mine, an apparition enthusiast, refused to dismiss these fruits and surmised, "I have close friends who have been to Medjugorje and their household is so peaceful, so loving, so prayerful and so spiritual. If they are deceived, I wish we had more deceived people in the world!" He may as well have expressed a desire that more people prophesy, cast out demons, and work miracles in Jesus' name. He may as well have wished that more people in the world would hear a false gospel and trust in their own works, or those of Mary, to gain entrance into Heaven. He may as well have wished that more people would trust in Mary as the 'greatest intercessor,' or that more people would give their lives 'to God through Our Lady.' He may as well have wished that more people would say "Lord, Lord" on Judgment Day only to hear Christ say in response, "I never knew you."

And every time I hear that another apparition of Mary has been sighted, every time I receive a copy of the most recent messages of the apparitions somewhere in the world, and every time I meet someone who wants me to visit one and see for myself, I am saddened that the Gospel continues to be withheld from so many. If my acquaintance wished that we had more deceived people in this world, his wish is coming true. And ultimately, Friar Ivan Dugandzic was right. Satan has resorted to prayer, fasting and conversion to Mary as a means of turning people from God. This clever deception has worked for centuries and Satan is understandably reluctant to abandon a method that has been so successful for him.

[†] 2 Timothy 3:15,16
[§] 1 Peter 3:15,16

Global Network

And many false prophets shall rise, and shall deceive many.
—*Matthew 24:11*

HAVING examined their fruits and teachings, I imagine that it would be rather difficult to proceed without actually proposing what I believe these numerous apparitions are really trying to do. Obviously, they are not Mary, and obviously they are lying about their identity and therefore are not from Heaven as they claim. But what option does that leave us? Is there some neutral spiritual middle ground between the angels of Heaven and the angels of hell? Is there something between the two that just enjoys acting on the peculiar beliefs of people, manifesting itself as whatever the people would like to see or would understand? Is there something between angels and demons that really means no harm, but no good either? If there is, I don't believe its description could be found in Scripture. The Word explains that some angels disobeyed God and were cast out. The rest remained in Heaven. There were none who simply chose not to decide.[179] Which means that if the apparitions of Mary do not come from the highest, holiest pinnacles of Heaven, we have no choice but to acknowledge that, in fact, they have their origins in the deepest, darkest recesses of the pits of hell. And since they teach a false gospel, we know quite simply that they are demonic. They may very well be the most prolific demonic manifestation of our times.

Now, I suppose that in reading the messages and considering the fruits of the many apparitions of Mary, one would begin to wonder if they were all really the same demon acting in so many

---

[179] See, among others, 2 Peter 2:4 and 1 Timothy 5:21

different places in the world, and to be quite honest, it is difficult to tell. Could one demon be so active in so many different locations? If not, has Satan been so clever as to coordinate such a complex, interrelated concert of alleged Marian appearances? He is certainly capable, but again, it is difficult to tell.

But we do have the testimony of the apparitions which seem to indicate that it is all a coordinated effort and may even be the work of one demon in particular. For example, when the apparition of Mary appeared to the children of Melleray Grotto, Ireland in 1985, it said, "I will show myself to more people in more places," and when it appeared again in Bessbrook Grotto, Ireland two years later, it made specific references to the Medjugorje apparitions: "The messages here are the messages in Medjugorje. The children in Medjugorje are the children here."[180] The apparition of Jesus in Conyers, Georgia, USA has made specific references to the Medjugorje apparitions,[181] while the apparition of Mary in Conyers has made implicit reference to the Rue de Bac apparitions by commanding Nancy Fowler to distribute Miraculous Medals on the hill behind her house.[182] Explicit reference has also been made to the Agreda apparitions by assigning the writings of Sister Mary of Agreda as reading material for Nancy.[183]

These cross references to other apparition locations are not uncommon, and when an apparition of Mary wishes to authenticate its appearances, it will often refer to previous apparition sites and messages to do so. Mary Ann Van Hoof of Necedah, Wisconsin, USA reported in 1950 that the apparition of Mary had told her that she was appearing in order to warn the people of the world "as I warned you at Fatima, Lipa [Philippines], and La Salette."[184] Likewise, when apparitions were reported in Amsterdam, Holland between 1945 and 1959, the defense of their authenticity was that they seemed to build upon the "eschatological landmarks" of the apparitions of LaSalette and

---

[180] Both quotes from *Our Lady Queen of Peace*, "Apparitions Europe," pg. 11. Used by permission
[181] *To Bear Witness*, pg. 64, para. 75. Message of December 4, 1990
[182] *To Bear Witness*, pg. 10
[183] *To Bear Witness*, pp. 65, 123
[184] Zimdars-Swartz, pg. 260. Brackets in original

Pontmain, France; Fátima, Portugal and Beauraing, Belgium,[185] all four of which had by then received the official approval of the Church. And when the apparition of Mary appeared to Estela Ruiz at Immaculate Heart Catholic Church in Phoenix, Arizona, USA, it said outright that all of these apparitions are the same person appearing in many different places:

> "Look around this church and see all the different forms in which I have appeared. I am the Mother of God and I have appeared in different places. There is only one and that is me and I am all of these."[186]

As it turned out, there were shrines and other such references to apparitions of Fátima, Guadalupe, and Our Lady of Sorrows there in the church. These and other explicit or implied references are recorded in tabular form in Table 3, on page 126. By 'explicit,' I mean that the apparition at one site refers to another apparition site by name; by 'implied,' I mean that the apparition has said something or done something that associates it with another site. For example, if the Conyers apparition had made references to the use of the Brown Scapular, I would have indicated a reference from Conyers to Mt. Carmel, the apparition of which was responsible for introducing that form of devotion.

From Table 3, it can be seen that there is a definite level of mutual reference and cooperation that we can infer from the apparitions' messages themselves. And while several apparitions have warned of demonic deceptions taking place in the world,[187] no apparition has ever identified another apparition site by name in that context. And in this manner, we can at least say that if the apparitions of Mary are all independent of each other, they are not suggesting it in any way. Whether the messages of one site are good or bad, the apparitions freely associate with one another and consistently suggest that they are all the work of the same spirit.

It is true, though, that the apparitions at one location might say something practically unheard of at another location, almost as if the apparition was opting to show a different personality at

---

[185] Zimdars-Swartz, pp. 256-7

[186] *Our Lady Queen of Peace*, "An Interview with Estela Ruiz," pg. 9. Used by permission

[187] See, for example, *To Bear Witness*, pp. 6-7

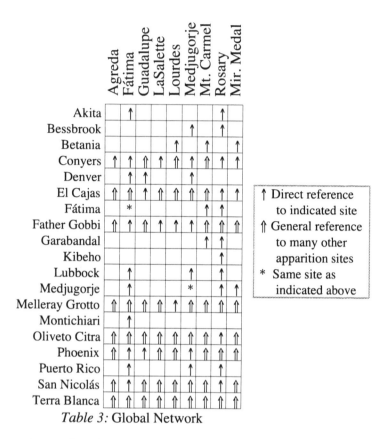

	Agreda	Fátima	Guadalupe	LaSalette	Lourdes	Medjugorje	Mt. Carmel	Rosary	Mir. Medal
Akita		↑						↑	
Bessbrook						↑		↑	
Betania				↑			↑		↑
Conyers	↑	↑	⇑	↑	⇑	↑	⇑	↑	↑
Denver		↑	↑			↑			
El Cajas	⇑	⇑	↑	⇑	⇑	⇑	⇑	↑	↑
Fátima		*					↑	↑	
Father Gobbi	⇑	↑	⇑	↑	↑	↑	⇑	⇑	⇑
Garabandal							↑	↑	
Kibeho								↑	
Lubbock		↑				↑		↑	
Medjugorje		↑				*		↑	↑
Melleray Grotto	⇑	⇑	⇑	⇑	↑	⇑	⇑	⇑	⇑
Montichiari		↑							
Oliveto Citra	⇑	⇑	⇑	⇑	⇑	⇑	⇑	↑	⇑
Phoenix	⇑	↑	↑	⇑	⇑	↑	⇑	⇑	⇑
Puerto Rico		↑				↑		↑	
San Nicolás	⇑	↑	⇑	⇑	⇑	⇑	⇑	↑	⇑
Terra Blanca	⇑	⇑	⇑	⇑	⇑	⇑	⇑	⇑	⇑

↑ Direct reference to indicated site
⇑ General reference to many other apparition sites
* Same site as indicated above

Table 3: Global Network

each location that it visits. For example, the standard message at Medjugorje has been, "Pray, fast and convert," but the messages received by the visionaries of Turzovka, Czechoslovakia in 1958 were of a very different tone:

> "All my children will receive and carry the sign of the cross on their foreheads. This sign only my chosen ones will see. These chosen ones will be instructed by my angels how to conduct themselves. My faithful will be without any kind of fear during the most difficult hours. They will be protected by the good spirits and will be fed by Heaven from where they will receive further instructions. They will fall into a deathlike sleep, but they will be protected by angels. When they awake they will be like newly born."

This message is comparatively unusual, but the apparition soon returned to the standard format by saying,

> "The angels who are entrusted with the work of destruction are ready, but the wrath of God can be stayed by praying the Rosary, by penance, and by the sinners(sic) repentance."[188]

In a similar manner, the apparitions at LaSalette began by threatening that the potato crop would fail and all of the children under seven years of age would die unless the town repented. But accompanying these apocalyptic threats was a simpler message that the children could understand and therefore could pass on to the adults: "If my people do not submit themselves, I must let the hand of my son fall upon them," and other statements emphasizing daily Mass and honoring the Lenten season.[189]

In the more recent occurrences, the apparition might make mention of a final ten year period of history in which mankind has a last opportunity to change its ways, as with Father Gobbi, the locutionist, or at Melleray Grotto, Ireland.[190] In another, it might say that the Heavenly Father has given the 20th century to Satan for him to persecute the Church, as in the messages of Medjugorje.[191] These statements don't necessarily conflict, but then, they aren't very similar either.

But in spite of whatever differences might be observed at various times and places, the apparitions tend to make certain statements that indicate a unity which might be otherwise obscured by the occasional variations. For example, the request for more sacrifices to pay for sins is almost universally present in the messages as is the promise of a "lasting sign." The apparition at Medjugorje has indicated that a "lasting sign" will appear near the town so that everyone will believe. A similar statement was made by the apparition at Garabandal, promising a permanent

---

[188] Both quotes from *Our Lady Queen of Peace*, "Apparitions: Europe--Far East," pg. 16. Used by permission

[189] Lord, pp. 70-2. Message of September 19, 1846

[190] *Our Lady Queen of Peace*, "Interior Locutions: From 1973 to the Present," pg. 6, message of September 18, 1988, and "Melleray Grotto, Ireland (1985)," pg. 11. Used by permission

[191] *Words from Heaven*, pg. 109

sign at the site where the children first saw the apparition of St. Michael. This promise was also given to Theresa Lopez by the apparition of Mary in Denver, Colorado.[192] Likewise, the Phenomenon of the Sun is very common and has been reported by pilgrims at Conyers, Denver, Lubbock, Fátima, Medjugorje, the Philippines, and other locations.

But whether the apparitions are one spirit, or a host of demons acting out the same drama in hundreds of locations, there is something very curious about their method. In many of the places that the apparitions visit they work miracles and teach falsehoods, to be sure, but there is something striking about the Phenomenon of the Sun, something that should catch the attention of every Christian. Recall that the apparition at Fátima seemed to make the sun come down and hover over the crowd that was gathered there. We know that it is physically impossible to make the sun come down to earth, but the 70,000 eyewitnesses that day in 1917 reported that their rain-soaked clothes dried out instantly when the sun plummeted toward them.[193] This phenomenon has occurred in many places associated with the apparitions, along with many cures, healings and other signs. And even though the vision isn't always as dramatic as it was in Fátima, witnesses still explain that the sun seems to spin, dance around in the sky, change to all the colors of the spectrum and then appear to come closer to earth and then move further away. This happened again before a crowd of 100,000 in Puerto Rico on April 23, 1991, which was the 38th anniversary of the apparitions there.[194]

It seems that everyone who has visited an apparition is told of this marvelous phenomenon, this dance of the sun. Considering this, along with the false gospel which the apparitions preach so consistently and the other miracles that are recorded, I would think that the next verse of Scripture would be of interest:

> "And I beheld another beast coming up out of the earth; and he had two horns like a lamb, and he spake as a dragon... And he doeth great wonders, so that he

---

[192] Kuntz, pg. 20

[193] Walsh, *Our Lady of Fátima*, pp. 146-7

[194] *Our Lady Queen of Peace*, "Our Lady of the Rosary in Puerto Rico," pg. 13. Used by permission

maketh fire come down from heaven on the earth in
the sight of men."[195]

If Jesus thought it was important enough to warn us about a
false prophet who would come to earth for the sole purpose of
deceiving the whole world, a false prophet who would perform
miracles with the intention of leading people astray, a false
prophet who would even make 'fire come down from heaven to
earth in the sight of everyone' in order to mislead them, then I
don't think it really matters if the apparitions are the work of one
demon or many. What matters is that they very well match the
description of a powerful force of evil that Jesus thought was of
enough concern to Him that he ought to warn us about it.

To these warnings, He also added,

> "For there shall arise false Christs, and false prophets,
> and shall shew great signs and wonders; insomuch that,
> if it were possible, they shall deceive the very elect."[196]

I realize that the chosen cannot be misled into damnation, but
Jesus' words here are curious: 'if that were possible.' The only
way someone could even attempt to mislead the elect or the
chosen would be to make sure that the signs and wonders used
were also accompanied by a gospel that almost seemed true. And
after all, the apparitions *do* talk about Jesus, His death on the
cross and His resurrection, but we also know that the gospel
which accompanies their many signs and wonders is a false one.

The reason I bring this up is to say that the Bible seems to
predict this specific type of false prophet, i.e., one who preaches
something very close to the truth accompanied by many signs and
wonders. That being the case, then, when we approach the
apparitions and study them, we ought to have at least a healthy
amount of respect for the demon behind them since their purpose
is to mislead even the chosen. Instead of approaching them with
an unhealthy curiosity for the demonic, we should be guarded in
Truth, lest we find ourselves hypnotized by the messages and
thereby becoming a source of misguidance and error, a stumbling
block, for others.

---

[195] Revelation 13:11,13
[196] Matthew 24:24

I understand that there is a natural curiosity that comes with being human, but there is serious cause for concern here. My fear is that curious Christians may wish to satisfy their intellect by visiting the actual locations of the apparitions, but I very strongly urge against this. This is very dangerous territory because whether the apparitions are one spirit or many spirits, they all have one common origin, and one common leader: Satan. He wants to lead people away from the true Jesus of the Bible and persuade them to place their trust and confidence elsewhere. He even wants to mislead the elect, 'if that were possible.'

If such a demon is dangerous for believers, how much more so for the unprotected? We should therefore keep our distance from the apparitions but stay in close contact with the victims because they, like so many other religious people in this world, have had the Gospel withheld from them and desperately need to hear the truth.

Beyond Silver and Gold

> Forasmuch as ye know that ye were not redeemed with corruptible things, as silver and gold, from your vain conversation received by tradition from your fathers; But with the precious blood of Christ, as of a lamb without blemish and without spot.
> —*1 Peter 1:18-19*

THE TRANSITION from being a religious person to being a Christian is not a small thing. When Christ was sharing the truth with unbelievers, he did so knowing that the people could not convert themselves any more than Peter could have understood the Gospel without the instruction of the Father:

> "And Jesus answered and said unto him, Blessed art thou, Simon Barjona: for flesh and blood hath not revealed it unto thee, but my Father which is in heaven."[197]

In the same way, the Gospel is not something that the flesh necessarily grasps or desires in itself. It is one thing to have a zeal for God, and quite another to have a zeal for God *according to knowledge*. This was Paul's concern with regard to his kinsmen as far as the flesh was concerned:

> "For I bear them record that they have a zeal of God, but not according to knowledge."[198]

---

[197] Matthew 16:17
[198] Romans 10:2

I think the reader can understand well enough that as a
Roman Catholic I had a zeal for goodness and even a zeal for
God—as I understood Him. But much like the myriad examples
given in an earlier chapter, "By Their Fruits," I was showing forth
a type of godliness that had nothing to do with the righteousness
of God. I was, like Paul's relatives, the unbelieving Jews,
captivated by a god of my own fashioning, paying homage in a
manner not revealed in the Bible. Instead, I was seeking to
establish my own righteousness:

> "For they being ignorant of God's righteousness, and
> going about to establish their own righteousness, have
> not submitted themselves unto the righteousness of
> God."[199]

Such was the condition of my heart as I sought after all
manner of Marian devotion, seeking after a god of my imagination and "going about to establish my own righteousness."
Perhaps the most difficult thing to imagine in all of this is that,
despite my great concern for godly living, and in spite of any
personal desire on my own for truth, I was dead in my sins,
unable either to help myself, or even to realize what is so apparent
to me now: *that I needed help.* I needed help, and much more than
that. Being dead in my sins, I needed someone who could raise
the dead. Someone Who could bring me out of death and into life.

What has become by far my most favorite parable in all of
Scripture is that of the Sower in Luke 8. Familiar as it may be to
those who have read it many times, there is something peculiar
about it that did not capture my attention at the first or even the
tenth reading. Christ summarizes the four different possible
results from the preaching of the Gospel, and of the four, there is
only one kind in which the Gospel actually takes root in the heart:

> "But that on the good ground are they, which in an
> honest and good heart, having heard the word, keep it,
> and bring forth fruit with patience."[200]

Two reasons—among others—that I considered this to be
such a remarkable parable are 1) that those who truly believe are

---

[199] Romans 10:3
[200] Luke 8:15

said to have received the word of God with "an honest and good heart," and 2) that the only thing which changes between the four different examples is the *soil*, and not the seed itself.

First, with only a little biblical research into the nature of man, it is clear that there is not one among us all who can claim to have been born with "an honest and good heart." Scripture completely rules this out, saying,

> "The heart is deceitful above all things, and desperately wicked: who can know it?"[201]

> "And God saw that the wickedness of man was great in the earth, and that every imagination of the thoughts of his heart was only evil continually."[202]

The significance of this in Jesus' parable of the Sower is that Jesus knew, as He did with Peter, that His listeners could not of themselves grasp what He was preaching, Christ knew that in order for His ministry to be effective in saving people, His Father would have to do something first. Only then could the Word He preached—that is, the seed He planted—take root in the heart. The heart had to be changed before the Gospel could be believed. This, as it turns out, is precisely what God says He does:

> "A new heart also will I give you, and a new spirit will I put within you: and I will take away the stony heart out of your flesh, and I will give you an heart of flesh."[203]

Second, Christ says that when the Sower preaches, He casts the *same* seed on all four different kinds of soils. This is extremely significant because it demonstrates to us exactly what should be at the center of our Gospel presentation to unbelievers: the Word. And always the Word. We need not try to accommodate the Gospel to different types of people by masking it in language they will be more open to, and we need not sugar-coat the Gospel to make it attractive or enticing to people. Rather, we should regard all men to have hearts of dead soil, faithfully

---

[201] Jeremiah 17:9
[202] Genesis 6:5
[203] Ezekiel 36:26

casting the Word of God on the soil, praying that the Lord will put *good* soil—the "honest and good heart" of Ezekiel 36:26—in them that they might believe the truth.

Accordingly, I must say that my own experience of changing from a religious person into a Christian was no small thing. It was a very large thing indeed—something a dead man could not do. Rather, a good many friends of mine obediently showered me with the Word of God, and by a supreme act of grace and power, God placed in me the only soil that could receive the implanted seed of the Word. A good number of other friends and acquaintances of mine had engaged me in doctrinal disputes about why the Rosary was wrong, and why the Pope is not infallible, and I argued point for point as a staunch Roman Catholic. But what won me over was not someone's clever argument or eloquent speaking. What made me believe the Gospel of Christ was the fact that God changed in me my heart of stone into a heart of flesh. And the Word of God, faithfully preached by friends and neighbors for years, for the first time in my life, took root and began to grow. The soil was finally good.

I bring this up to make a specific point—to explain why I *didn't* write this book: I didn't write this book to bash Catholic doctrines. As you know, I have yet to criticize the doctrines at all. At the most, I have assumed them to be true! And I didn't write this book to make fun of the Rosary or the Scapular or anything specifically Catholic at all.

There is no shortage of books that address the traditions and theologies of the Catholic Church, and I do not wish at this time to contribute to the surplus. And much of the criticism I have heard has been directed at the Rosary and the veneration of Mary, but only in the sense that these forms of devotion seemed strange. The problem is that it is admittedly difficult to argue such matters with those who are taught to trust solely in the instructions handed down to them from the Church. And far be it from Christians to argue on this basis in the first place, because there is nothing as unbelievable and strange to natural men as the notion that an innocent God would come down to Earth, die in our place, allow Himself to be treated as if He was guilty, and then say that in spite of our rebellion, He has provided a way for us to come back. To the natural man, this is not logical but it is true. Human reasoning would never have allowed for this exchange or arrived at this conclusion, so it is not always the best course of action when trying to introduce people to Christ.

Now I do believe that the Rosary is a problem, along with the veneration of Mary and the wearing of the Scapular and the Miraculous Medal, but these are only symptoms of a much deeper issue: people who feel a need to be reconciled to God, but still try other-than-prescribed methods of doing so. That is, they believe that the Rosary, the Scapular and the Medal will help them be reconciled to God, and they fail to understand that Christ was sent to be *the* Mediator between God and man: the Reconciler of all creation. But in their blindness, and in their desperation, they have inserted yet another link between God and man: Mary.

It was through Satan's work and deception that Adam rebelled and made us all unworthy of approaching God directly. God corrected the problem so that even though our sin prevented us from approaching Him directly, we could still come directly to His Son, and Jesus could go directly to God for us.

That solved our dilemma, but the issue of the veneration of Mary is that the new theology says, "You are not good enough to come to Jesus, but you can come directly to Mary and she can go directly to Jesus on your behalf." Thus we have the new Catholic intercessory theology: 'Through Mary to Jesus,'[204] and it is in this manner that many Catholics approach God. I quote from a pamphlet circulated by Medjugorje enthusiasts:

> "Of all the archangels, including Michael and Raphael, all the angels, all the prophets, including Abraham, Moses, and Elijah, and all the human race put together, no one has been as close to God as Mary. She is not a deity. Her place with God is above all angels and all mankind but below God. BETWEEN. ...Just as Our Lady's role is not on an equal basis with any angel or man but above their roles and below God's, Her role is to lead us to God."[205]

As you can see, the real problem is the development of a new barrier between God and man, a barrier which only Mary can overcome. Thus she becomes, as you have read, redemptress and mediatrix. As the apparition has said, it places itself as mediatrix

---

[204] *Blue Army Cell Manual*, ©AMI Press, Blue Army of Our Lady of Fátima, Washington, New Jersey, 07882, pg. 18

[205] *Understanding Our Lady's Messages*, pp. 13-14. Emphasis in original

between God and mankind, or between Jesus and mankind. This chain of intercession was carried one step further in Garabandal, Spain, as the last message from the apparition there was delivered, not by Mary, but from Mary "through the intercession of St. Michael the Archangel," because, "my message of October 18th, [1961] has not been complied with and has not been made known to the world." Mary, so it seemed, was tired of being ignored, and this was to be her last message.[206]

The extrapolations from this point could be endless. If Mary grows impatient with us, then perhaps we can approach Michael, whose role it is to lead us to an angry Mary. He can safely approach Mary, who can safely approach an angry Jesus, who can approach God, the Father. And so on... But what if Michael became angry with us? To whom would we go? Thankfully, we need have no fear of just going directly through Jesus, for it is written that this was God's plan to begin with:

> "According to the eternal purpose which he purposed
> in Christ Jesus our Lord: In whom we have boldness
> and access with confidence by the faith of him.

This method of mediation from man through Jesus Christ to the Father is the only one that God has established in His Word, and therefore communications to Him through the methods prescribed by the apparitions are wholly ineffective.

This is the same problem with *anyone* who has not trusted in Jesus Christ alone by faith alone to be Redeemer and Mediator. Someone who trusts in Mary as redemptress and mediatrix is just as deceived as someone who trusts in St. Michael or even in themselves in that role. Isn't it natural for humans to picture themselves explaining to God why He should allow them into Heaven? This is almost second nature to us, but trusting in Mary to do this is just as pointless. The fact is that the barrier that now exists between God and man is so large that it cannot be overcome by anyone but Jesus. But the way to help the deceived is not to ridicule their trust in Mary—the best way to reach people who have devoted their lives to Mary is to share the Gospel, because only then will they see what has been lacking. If one does

---

[206] "Marian Apparitions of the 20th Century: A Message of Urgency." Message of June 18, 1965. Brackets added for clarity

not understand the unique position Christ has in reconciling man to God, one will not recognize the fundamental deception in allowing anyone else to play that role.

The reason I bring all of this up is to prepare the reader for what I am about to say. But first I want to preface it with another comment: the only people who will go to Heaven are those who have trusted Jesus Christ *alone* by faith alone for their eternal salvation. This may seem too simple, but it is what the Bible teaches:

> "Neither is there salvation in any other: for there is none other name under heaven given among men, whereby we must be saved."[207]

Again, the only people who will go to Heaven are those who have trusted Jesus Christ *alone* by faith alone for their salvation.

And for that matter, the only Baptists who will go to Heaven are those who have trusted Jesus Christ *alone* by faith alone for their salvation.

The only Methodists who will go to Heaven are those who have trusted Jesus Christ *alone* by faith alone for their salvation.

The only Charismatics who will go to Heaven are those who have trusted Jesus Christ *alone* by faith alone for their salvation.

The only Presbyterians who will go to Heaven are those who have trusted Jesus Christ *alone* by faith alone for their salvation.

The only Anglicans who will go to Heaven are those who have trusted Jesus Christ *alone* by faith alone for their salvation.

The only people who will go to Heaven are those who have trusted Jesus Christ *alone* by faith alone for their salvation.

And so on, and so on...

The only way anyone can get to Heaven is if they have trusted Jesus Christ *alone* by faith alone for their eternal salvation.

Why do I say this? Because if I did not emphasize that specific point, my next statement would be considered offensive:

> The only Catholics who will go to Heaven are those who have trusted Jesus Christ *alone* by faith alone for their eternal salvation.

Which means that any Catholics who put their trust in Mary and Jesus, or in Mary alone, have not trusted Jesus *alone*, and are

---

[207] Acts 4:12

doomed to hell. And for that matter, any Baptists who trust in Mary and Jesus, or in Mary alone, have not trusted Jesus *alone* to reconcile them to the Father, and are doomed to hell. And so on, and so on...

Which means that the millions of people who have visited the apparition sites around the world and henceforth have trusted Mary, whether in union with Jesus or in Mary alone, have put their trust in someone who cannot save them. The millions of people who have gone on pilgrimages to Fátima, Lourdes, Conyers, Medjugorje, Phoenix, Denver, Lubbock, etc... have all placed their trust in something that is not even Mary, *and who can do nothing to save them at all*. As has already been discussed, these apparitions are demonic. They are from the pit of hell and they want nothing more than to deceive people into trusting anyone but Jesus. And for all the apparition cares, you can put your trust in anyone *but Jesus alone*, and it will be satisfied. This is why the apparition emphasizes mediation through Mary to Jesus to the Father, or just through Mary to the Father. But the apparition will never, ever emphasize a path of salvation from sinful man through Jesus *only*, to the Father. Why? Because that's the *only* method the Bible teaches, and none other.

I am now informed that there is a woman who is receiving interior locutions about Medjugorje directly from the Eternal Father, *with no mediation at all*.[208] This is so fundamentally inconsistent with Scripture that I was surprised that the editor of *Our Lady Queen of Peace* allowed it into the final publication. But it only serves to illustrate my point. The messages of the apparitions of Mary are summarized in this: "Please, *please* trust in anyone in the whole world, any*thing*, any *person*, any *saint*, any*body*, anyone at all as your mediator between you and God. Even yourself. But whatever you do, please, *please* do not put your trust *solely* in the Jesus Christ of the Bible." Because if you do, the apparition's mission will have failed. And it doesn't want to fail. It wants people to keep it company for an eternity in hell.

So how shall we reach the people who have been deceived by the apparitions of Mary? I advise you to avoid the methods that did not work on me. If you try only to tell them how wrong Catholic doctrines are without also lovingly sprinkling the Word

---

[208] *Our Lady Queen of Peace*, "The Eternal Father Speaks to a Stigmatist in Montreal," pg. 10. Used by permission

on their hearts, they will likely respond in the same manner that I did—they will be driven back to their devotion to Mary with more fervency and strength than ever. But there is something that works: the Word. Tell them the True Gospel. Immerse them in the Word of God. Cast the seed of the Word on the soil of their hearts. Invite them to a Bible study or start one yourself. Give them the Word. Bathe them in it, shower them in it, pour it on their heads and on their feet until they are drowning in it and it oozes from their very pores and testifies to the transforming power of God's written message to mankind. That, in concert with prayer, is the only way to bring someone successfully out of devotion to Mary and the apparitions. That is what brought me out of devotion to Mary, and I will spend my eternity praising the Name of the Living God for the people He sent my way to show me the truth. To show me Jesus. To show me the Word.

Anything less would have failed miserably.

Association

Can the blind lead the blind? shall they not both
fall into the ditch?
—Luke 6:39

I F I WERE a visitor in a small suburban church and I wished
to address the congregation there, I believe I would try to
contact the pastor of that local body of believers and
somehow get in good graces with him before approaching the
congregation with my message. This is an important step since it
is the pastor who is responsible for the spiritual health and well-
being of all the members of his fold. They have all been placed in
his care and he is responsible for their spiritual growth and is
ultimately accountable for whatever teaching reaches their ears.
So in the interest of gaining the attention of the congregation
members, I would first acquaint myself with the man whom God
had appointed as their shepherd. In doing so, I would be assured
that the people to whom I spoke would have some degree of
confidence that whatever I said had the approval of the man to
whom they had chosen to submit.

And this notion applies to all walks of life. If I wanted to
address a high school student body, I would seek the favor of the
principal of that high school. If I wished to present something to a
corporate work force, I would first try to gain the approval of the
president of the company.

Because this is so basic and so intuitive, one should not find it
surprising that the apparitions of Mary have not merely gone to
the Catholic people without at least on the side trying to curry the
approval of the papacy, under whom Catholics everywhere
receive their proper teaching. And it makes sense. Since the
Vatican ultimately has the power to approve or disapprove the
authenticity of paranormal or supernatural events, the instigator of

such events would hardly wish to offend the papacy by preaching insurrection and general disobedience to the Chair of St. Peter. Quite the contrary. One would do nothing short of emphasizing the importance of listening, above all else, to the teachings of the Church leaders and submitting to them. These are both solid Biblical principles of Church life, and the Church recognizes this.

The Catholic Almanac contains a brief summary of the conditions which must be met in order for an apparition to be approved by the Church, one of which states implicitly that apparitions which stir up dissent in the Body of Christ or "produce any sentiment of contempt toward anyone," will not be looked upon favorably.[209] It is for this reason that the apparition of St. Michael the Archangel stopped administering the Holy Eucharist to the children of Garabandal, Spain, except when there were no priests in the village. After all, St. Michael, though frequently in the presence of God, was not ordained as a priest and therefore could not perform the function of one, i.e., to consecrate the bread and wine and perform the actual rite of transubstantiation. When the local priests felt that their positions were being usurped, the apparition of St. Michael immediately honored their concerns and only administered the Eucharist to the children when no other priests were available,[210] and only then with already-consecrated hosts that he had taken from a tabernacle somewhere else on earth.[211] Anything less than this immediate response would have been viewed unfavorably by the Church, and especially by the investigation committee whose responsibility it was to determine if the apparitions at Garabandal were from God.

This being the case, it is no surprise that the apparition has spoken very favorably of the pastor of the Catholic Church: "The priests must follow the pope for to walk by him is to walk by my Son Himself."[212] Statements like this one are to be found in the recorded messages of almost every apparition in the world and

---

[209] *1993 Catholic Almanac*, Felician A. Roy, ed., (Huntington, IN: Our Sunday Visitor Publishing Division, Our Sunday Visitor, Inc., ©1992), "Criteria of Apparitions," pg. 265

[210] "Marian Apparitions of the 20th Century: A Message of Urgency"

[211] Zimdars-Swartz, pg. 141

[212] *Our Lady Queen of Peace*, "An Urgent Appeal: Our Lady in Argentina," pg. 7. Message of October 27, 1986. Used by permission

they all have made it clear that they defer great weight to the interests of the papacy. Such messages as these make it very clear that the apparition knows to whom it should go for approval.

But what concerns me is not so much whether the apparitions address the issue of the Church hierarchy properly as much as why the apparitions are so comfortable doing so in the first place. And why the papacy has been so receptive to the messages.

The apparitions have urged the visionaries from the beginning to forward messages to the pope, whether from the apparition at LaSalette to Pius IX in 1846, or more recently from the apparition at Medjugorje to John Paul II in 1983:

> "You must inform the bishop and the Pope with respect to the urgent and great importance of the message for all mankind."[213]

And like the secret message of LaSalette, the apparition at Medjugorje has at least once had the visionaries forward a confidential message to John Paul II. This information comes from a diary of a pilgrim to Medjugorje. She refers to a question and answer session with one of the visionaries:

> "My questions to Maria(sic) were: 'Has Our Lady given a message to Our Holy Father?' 'Yes,' she replied. 'Well, what was it?' I asked. 'It is for him,' she answered smilingly. 'Oh,' and the whole crowd laughed. 'It was a personal message for him,' she explained."[214]

But the great lengths to which the apparitions of Mary have gone in catering to the interests of the papacy are not without reason. The apparition, by establishing a certain working trust with the papacy, has secured for itself what could be considered a 'most favored' status, and it has done so with each pontificate with which it chooses to interact. The apparitions have not been secret about their affection for the papacy, and the papacy in return has been far from secretive about its warm relations with the apparitions. Pope after pope has generously reciprocated these

---

[213] *Caritas of Birmingham*, January-April 1991 edition, pp. 13-14. Message of November 30, 1983

[214] Graham, Anna, *Diary of a Pilgrim to Medjugorje*, December 4, 1988, pg. 8

favors which the apparitions bestow. For example, the papacy has often shown its genuine approval of the apparitions of Mary by placing expensive gifts on statues which honor them. This is apparent in Pope Pius XII's proclamation calling for a worldwide veneration of Mary:

> "In the encyclical which His Holiness promulgated for the Institution of the Queenship of Mary in St. Peter's Basilica in Rome, climaxing a world-wide 'Marian Year'... the Holy Father recalled that he had already 'crowned her Queen of the World at Fatima.' His Holiness said: 'We may especially call to mind the radio message which we addressed to the people of Portugal when the miraculous image of the Virgin Mary which is venerated at Fatima, was being crowned with a golden diadem.'"[215]

And crown her he did, when he sent a Cardinal Legate to Fátima with a $500,000 crown to place on a statue of Mary on May 13, 1946.[216]

This happened again at the Shrine of Our Lady in Knock, Ireland. In 1879, an apparition visited Knock, and though it remained silent during the entire visit, more than 687 cures were documented during the first year after the incident. The Knock apparitions have yet to be officially approved by the Church, but the pope has not withheld his own personal approval:

> "Perhaps the greatest endorsement of our Lady's visit to Knock, Ireland, came from His Holiness, Pope John Paul II in 1979, for the Centenary. He came as a pilgrim to Knock. He celebrated Mass in the Basilica, anointed the sick, and went to the shrine to pray. He also presented to Knock Shrine a gold rose, in commemoration of the gold rose that Mary wore during her apparition."[217]

John Paul II has not withheld his personal approval of the Medjugorje apparitions, either. Though he defers to the judgment

---

[215] *Blue Army Cell Manual*, pg. 3, from AAS 38(1946)

[216] Haffert, John M., *Russia Will Be Converted*, (Washington, NJ: AMI International Press, ©1950) pp. 116-7

[217] Lord, pp. 125-6

of the council which was set up to determine the apparition's authenticity, he states, "If I wasn't a Pope I'd be in Medjugorje already!"[218]

In addition to these gifts and affirmations, the papacy has used its authority to perpetuate the ritual wearing of the Brown Scapular of Our Lady of Mt. Carmel and the praying of the Rosary, both of these traditions having been given to the Church by the apparitions of Mary. In the text of his infallible statement, *Munificentissimus Deus*, Pius XII emphasized the praying of "the Rosary of Mary, the recitation of which this Apostolic See so urgently recommends."[219] Further, when Pope Paul VI addressed the International Marian Congress in 1967, he said:

> "You will make known our will and our exhortations which we base upon the dogmatic constitution of the Ecumenical Council Vatican II, which is in complete conformity with our thought and indeed upon which our thought is based: 'That one ever hold in great esteem the practices and exercises of the devotion to the most blessed Virgin which have been recommended for centuries by the Magisterium of the Church.' And among them we judge well to recall especially the Marian Rosary and the religious use of the Scapular of Mount Carmel...a form of piety which is adapted by its simplicity to the spirit indeed of everyone, and is most largely widespread among the faithful for an increase of spiritual fruit."[220]

And when the Fátima apparition wanted the popes to consecrate Russia and the rest of the world to the Immaculate Heart of Mary, the papacy was quick to respond. The 1917 apparition made a promise during a visit that year, a promise that was conditioned upon papal compliance with the apparition's request. The Fátima visionary, Lucia Abóbora, relates:

> "What Our Lady wants is that the Pope and all the bishops in the world shall consecrate Russia to her

---

[218] Ashton, pg. 216

[219] Pope Pius XII, *Munificentissimus Deus*, AAS 42(1950):758

[220] *Blue Army Cell Manual*, pp. 9-10. Paul VI quotes from Pius XII, Epistle *Neminem Profecto Latet*, AAS 42(1950):390

Immaculate Heart on one special day. If this is done,
she will convert Russia and there will be peace."[221]

Pope Pius XII attempted to fulfill the apparition's requests on
July 7, 1952 when he consecrated the world "and particularly the
Russian people" to the Immaculate Heart of Mary, but apparently
it was not done in union with the bishops of the world and
therefore was not in strict compliance with the original mandate.
Pope Paul VI attempted this again in 1964 and consecrated the
world to the Immaculate Heart of Mary, but did not mention
Russia, and therefore failed to comply with the instructions of the
apparition as well. John Paul II tried yet again on May 13, 1982
and even united himself "in intention" with all the bishops of the
world to consecrate the world to the Immaculate Heart of Mary,
but Russia was only mentioned as a part of the consecration and
was not the focus of it. Therefore his efforts fell just short of
accommodating the Fátima request.[222] But on March 25, 1984 in
St. Peter's Square in Rome, John Paul II performed the
consecration exactly as the Fátima apparition requested and said,

> "The act requested at Fátima is now accomplished, but
> now it is necessary for every bishop to consecrate his
> own diocese, every pastor his own parish, every father
> and mother their own family."[223]

There are still some who believe that John Paul II's latest
consecration was not valid either, but his efforts, along with those
of his predecessors, make one thing very clear: the papacy and the
apparitions have been very cooperative with each other to the
point of developing a public and interactive familiarity between
themselves. The apparition wants a public consecration to Mary's
Immaculate Heart—the papacy makes one. The apparition intro-
duces a ritual—the papacy approves it. The apparition instructs us
to follow the pope—the papacy responds in kind, teaching that we

---

[221] Walsh, *Our Lady of Fátima*, pg. 221

[222] *Our Lady of Fatima's Peace Plan from Heaven*, (Rockford, IL:
TAN Books and Publishers, Inc., ©1983) pg. 13

[223] *Signs of the Times*, Volume 6, Number 1, January/February/March
1994, "Bishop Hnilica Calls for Global Consecration to the Immaculate
Heart of Mary: 'Her Triumph is Now at the Door...,'"pp. 32-34

should follow Mary. But this mutual interaction reaches its most dramatic level when one considers the development of the Marian doctrines of the Catholic Church. The doctrines of the Immaculate Conception of Mary and of the Assumption of Mary were discussed earlier in this book with the understanding that the papacy was solely responsible for proclaiming them. But what becomes clear in a study of the doctrines is that the apparitions were largely responsible for urging—even insisting—that the papacy make the proclamations. In that light, it becomes clear that while the apparitions build up the authority of the papacy in their messages, the papacy in return has established the validity of the apparitions and has given them a certain authority of their own. The apparitions' long-standing affirmation of the authority of the papacy has indeed paid off.

As you will recall, in 1830 the apparition instructed Catherine Labouré to manufacture and distribute the Miraculous Medal, the imprint on which made explicit reference to Mary's Immaculate Conception. This would mean very little were it not for the fact that the Immaculate Conception had not yet been established as doctrine by Pope Pius IX, and would not be for another 24 years. And when the doctrine was finally proclaimed in 1854, it was understood that the apparition had not only played its role in the definition of the doctrine, but had also influenced the outcome of the Church's investigation into the visions:

> "While it is generally acknowledged that the great popularity of this 'Miraculous Medal' helped prepare the way for Pope Pius IX's proclamation of the dogma of the Immaculate Conception in 1854, it would seem that it also contributed substantially to the Church's formal approval of the authenticity of Catherine's visions."[224]

And when the Immaculate Conception doctrine at first met with skepticism, the apparition was quick to lend its support. Only four years after Pius IX proclaimed the doctrine, the apparition appeared again, this time in Lourdes, France, to a young girl named Bernadette Soubirous. During the first encounter when the apparition was asked its identity, it responded by saying "I am the Immaculate Conception," a statement which Bernadette would quickly relate to her priest and a claim which would in the eyes of

---

[224] Zimdars-Swartz, pg. 26

many provide the confirmation the doctrine desperately needed in order to be universally accepted:

> "The dogma of the Immaculate Conception of the Blessed Virgin Mary was of some political importance to nineteenth-century Catholicism... [It] was to most people as unapproachable as the idea of the Trinity itself... Nevertheless, enthusiasm for the baffling new dogma was an important part of the French clergy's attempts to lead a nineteenth-century religious revival. Bernadette could hardly have provided... a more welcome, or a more unexpected, name."[225]

And so it was that the apparition of Mary, by confirming the validity of the Immaculate Conception, assured that the 'baffling new dogma' would be accepted by the people quickly and without further question. This resulted in a general feeling of confidence in the ability of the papacy to establish truth, and the doctrine of Papal Infallibility was well on its way—a doctrine to which the apparitions would also lend their support.

It was not until 1870 that the doctrine of Papal Infallibility would be defined by Vatican Council I, but Pope Pius IX had had infallibility on his mind since 1846. It was during that year that the apparition of Mary, this time in LaSalette, France, appeared to Maximin Giraud and Melanie Mathieu and asked them to forward a secret to the pope. Very little is known of that secret, save that it contained two very important words. The children, though sworn to secrecy by the apparition, knew neither the spelling nor the meaning of "infallibly" and "pontiff," and therefore had to ask about them out loud before they could be written down.[226] The rest of the text is unknown except to the very few who have actually seen it, but when the message was forwarded to Pius IX, the hint was clear enough and the doctrine was on its way to a formal proclamation by the Magisterium of the Church.

Twenty-four years later on February 12, 1870, just months before Vatican Council I would proclaim the doctrine, Pope Pius IX received visionary Don Bosco in a private audience. Bosco

---

[225] Marnham, Patrick, *Lourdes: A Modern Pilgrimage*, (New York: Coward, McCann & Geoghegan, Inc., ©1980) pp. 4, 8-9. Brackets added for clarity

[226] Zimdars-Swartz, pp. 177-9

had received certain revelations about the advancement of the doctrine of Papal Infallibility and needed desperately to relate the vision to the pope. His vision provided instructions and directions for Pius IX to proceed with the doctrine even if he had only two bishops supporting him. Regardless of the circumstances, the pope could count on Mary's protection and guidance. The vision was spoken in mystical allegories, but with Bosco's assistance in interpreting the meanings, and in light of Pius IX's earlier secret from the apparition at LaSalette, the message was quite clear (Bosco's own annotations are shown in parentheses):

> "Now the voice of Heaven is addressed to the Shepherd of Shepherds. *(To Pius IX.)* You are in solemn conference with your co-workers *(the Vatican Council)*, but the enemy of good never stands idle... Hurry! If knots cannot be untied, sever them. Do not halt in the face of difficulties, but go forth until the hydra of error has been beheaded *(through the proclamation of the dogma of papal infallibility)...* Gather around you only two co-workers, yet wherever you go, carry on the task entrusted to you and bring it to completion *(the Vatican Council).* ...the great Queen shall always assist you, and, as in the past, She shall always be the powerful, prodigious defense of the Church."[227]

When Pius IX finally did proceed with the new doctrine of Papal Infallibility, he did so at the insistence of the apparition, and based the Infallibility dogma on the foundation he had already laid earlier with the Immaculate Conception proclamation. Thus, the declaration of his infallibility would be a mere formality:

> "People want to credit me with infallibility. I don't need it at all. Am I not infallible already? Didn't I establish the dogma of the Virgin's Immaculate Conception all by myself several years ago?"[228]

[227] *Dreams, Visions & Prophecies of Don Bosco*, Brown, Eugene M., editor, (New Rochelle, NY: Don Bosco Publications, ©1986) pg. 114. Parentheses in original

[228] Hasler, August Bernhard, *How the Pope Became Infallible: Pius IX and the Politics of Persuasion*, (New York: Doubleday & Company, Inc., ©1981) pg. 82

He did establish it indeed, but not without the assistance of the apparition. The history of the Immaculate Conception doctrine indicates that from start to finish it had been heavily influenced by the apparitions of Mary. The Papal Infallibility doctrine shared a similar history. The apparition suggested the doctrine of Papal Infallibility in 1846, and then returned the year Infallibility was finally proclaimed and assured Pius IX that he was on the correct course. With these two doctrines secure, the papacy was able to make its next official proclamation on Mary.

In 1950 Pope Pius XII proclaimed the doctrine of the Assumption of Mary, but did so by appealing to the two doctrines that the apparitions had helped Pius IX establish: the Immaculate Conception of Mary and the Infallibility of the Pope. In the preamble to the proclamation of the new dogma, Pius XII referred both to Mary, who was "immaculate in her conception," and to the authority of the Papacy, which was "infallibly" directed to proclaim such a doctrine.[229] Thus, the Assumption rested on two very significant pillars that the apparition had helped erect, pillars which simultaneously demanded the proclamation of the dogma and made the proclamation possible: Mary was assumed into Heaven *because* she was immaculate, and the papacy could proclaim the Assumption *because* it was infallible.

This may at first seem to be a tremendous and even unnecessary amount of effort for the apparitions to exert just to see these doctrines established, but without them the apparitions of Mary have no justification for their appearances. They simply could not be appearing *bodily* from Heaven were it not for the Assumption doctrine which stated explicitly that Mary had been taken *body* and soul into Heaven when she left the earth. Without this critical doctrine, the apparition would be at a loss to explain how it could be physically appearing to us prior to the general resurrection. Indeed, Mary's assumption into Heaven was the singular exception and was 'contrary to the general law' which would have otherwise made such bodily appearances impossible:

> "When we say that Our Lady was assumed into heaven, we mean that [it was] contrary to the general law by which the bodies of the faithful are condemned

---

[229] Pope Pius XII, *Munificentissimus Deus*, AAS 42(1950):761

> to corruption and to the earth until the time of the
> general judgment."[230]

If Mary had not been excepted from this law, then the
apparition could not justify its bodily appearances since Mary's
body, like the rest of 'the bodies of the faithful,' would still be in
the grave awaiting Judgment Day, making the appearances an
impossibility. The apparition *needed* the doctrines so that there
would be a logical explanation for its physical interaction with the
visionaries, and the circular means by which it obtained them
from the papacy is shown graphically on page 151.

And scarcely had the papacy proclaimed the Assumption than
the apparition was beginning a new campaign for the final Marian
dogma to be announced. The apparition of Mary in Amsterdam
from 1945 to 1959 insisted to visionary Ida Peederman that it was
time for the Church "to go further than it had yet gone. In these
last days, with the forces of Satan gathering to do battle with
Mary and her followers, it was time... for the Church to proclaim
her, as she had asked, 'Co-Redemptrix, Mediatrix, and Advocate.'"[231]

The road from Amsterdam to Rome has not been a long one.
This movement in support of proclaiming the final doctrine of
Mary is still strong and gaining support today. Bishop Paolo
Hnilica writes,

> "I hope that 1994 introduces us... into the age of the
> Triumph of Mary. It is in this light that we should
> work so that the final dogma of Mary, Co-Redemptrix,
> Mediatrix of All Graces, and Advocate, may be
> proclaimed as soon as possible. ...innumerable faith-
> ful, priests, and many bishops sense the need to honor
> Our Lady fully, recognizing the role that Her Son has
> given Her for all the Church Universal: Mother, Co-
> Redemptrix, and Mediatrix of All Graces."[232]

---

[230] Carter, G. E., "The Assumption of the Blessed Virgin," *Studia
Mariana: Vers le dogma de l' Assomption,* 4: 425-32, Montreal, 1948
(As quoted in Duggan, pg. 42). Brackets added for clarity
[231] Zimdars-Swartz, pp. 257-8
[232] *Signs of the Times*, Volume 6, Number 1, January/February/March
1994. "Bishop Hnilica Calls for Global Consecration to the Immaculate
Heart of Mary: 'Her Triumph is Now at the Door...,'" pp. 32-34

Circular Development of the Marian Doctrines

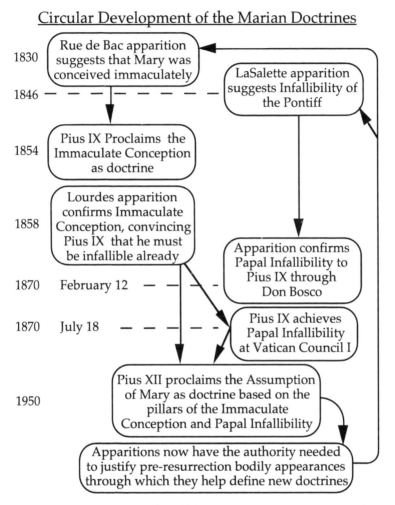

1830 — Rue de Bac apparition suggests that Mary was conceived immaculately

LaSalette apparition suggests Infallibility of the Pontiff

1846

1854 — Pius IX Proclaims the Immaculate Conception as doctrine

1858 — Lourdes apparition confirms Immaculate Conception, convincing Pius IX that he must be infallible already

Apparition confirms Papal Infallibility to Pius IX through Don Bosco

1870 — February 12

1870 — July 18

Pius IX achieves Papal Infallibility at Vatican Council I

1950 — Pius XII proclaims the Assumption of Mary as doctrine based on the pillars of the Immaculate Conception and Papal Infallibility

Apparitions now have the authority needed to justify pre-resurrection bodily appearances through which they help define new doctrines

Perhaps the papacy will respond again to the requests of the apparitions as it has in the past. Hnilica is the Titular Bishop of Rusado and is an itinerant clergyman whose home base is Rome. He has conversed with John Paul II on such matters as these on other occasions,[233] so if Hnilica needs support for the doctrine, he doubtlessly has the pope's ear. And if he doesn't, there is one proponent of the doctrine who does: Luigi Cardinal Ciappi, O.P.,

---

[233] *Signs of the Times*, Volume 6, Number 1, pp. 32-34

Papal Theologian Emeritus for John Paul II and for every pope
since Pius XII who proclaimed the doctrine of the Assumption of
Mary. Ciappi was the professor of Mariology for John Paul II
when he was still in school, and Ciappi has one last assignment
for his student:

> "With the profound contribution of our present Holy
> Father, Pope John Paul II, to the understanding of the
> mediating mystery of Mary with Christ and the Church
> ...there is only one final action that remains in
> bringing the Marian roles of Coredemptrix, Mediatrix
> and Advocate ...into the fullest acknowledgment and
> ecclesial life of the People of God: that our Holy
> Father, in his office as Vicar of Christ on earth and
> guided by the Spirit of Truth, define and proclaim the
> Marian roles of Coredemptrix, Mediatrix of all graces,
> and Advocate for the People of God as *Christian
> dogma* revealed by God, in rightful veneration of the
> Mother of Jesus, and for the good of the one, holy,
> catholic and apostolic Church of Christ."[234]

Even Mother Teresa joined in the effort to see this new doctrine proclaimed. She wrote, "Mary is our Advocate who prays to
Jesus for us. It is only through the Heart of Mary that we come to
the Eucharistic Heart of Jesus. The papal definition of Mary as
Coredemptrix, Mediatrix, and Advocate will bring great graces to
the Church."[235] She seemed confident, as do the dogma's many
other proponents, that the Pope will soon see the light and
proclaim the doctrine as a matter of obligatory faith for Catholics.
Mother Teresa's confidence was justified. The apparitions have
proven already that they are capable of using the papacy to
establish doctrine almost at will. After such successes as Papal
Infallibility, Mary's Immaculate Conception and the Assumption,
this final doctrine should pose no great difficulty to the apparition.
     But the final doctrine does pose a great difficulty to the
simplicity of the Gospel of Jesus Christ, and in that light we can

---

[234] Miravalle, Mark I., S.T.D., *Mary: Coredemptrix, Mediatrix,
Advocate*, (Santa Barbara, CA: Queenship Publishing, ©1993) pg. ix.
The words actually belong to Miravalle, but Ciappi quoted them in his
forward to Miravalle's book as they appear here. Emphasis in original
[235] *Signs of the Times*, Volume 5, Number 4, September/October/
November 1993, "Marian News Update," pg. 7

see clearly the true purpose of the apparition. If and when the final dogma is proclaimed, it will represent the complete transfer of all of the messianic attributes of Christ to Mary, or rather, to the apparition that claims to be Mary: His sinlessness, His resurrection, His role as Redeemer, Mediator and Advocate. One has to wonder why Mary would have any interest in such honors, but for the apparition, a transfer of these honors is essential. For all practical purposes the final Marian doctrine would not only make salvation through Christ alone obsolete but would also make it possible to call oneself 'Christian' without even the smallest understanding of Christ's unique role in redemption. The transfer of these messianic attributes to Mary would make the Biblical Gospel of Jesus Christ an impotent, historical artifact from a time when salvation was too simple, and too pure, from a time when people who were just too familiar with the Scriptures to be fooled.

And the Gospel really must be the core issue in any discussion regarding the true identity of the apparitions. The central issue really is not a matter of how much money is spent on expensive crowns and golden roses or what articles people wear to show their devotion, or even a matter of how much affection the papacy has toward Mary. After all, Mary was an excellent model of submission and obedience who should inspire all Christians, and if it really was Mary who was appearing, she would certainly have words worth listening to. Rather, the real issue is what the apparitions are teaching, and how the papacy views their messages:

> "As Cardinal Tedeschini said when he came to Fatima
> as legate of Pius XII in 1951: 'Fatima is an affirmation
> of the gospel.'"[236]

But when the apparition claims that the Rosary and the Brown Scapular can assure salvation, the question I have is, "Which gospel is the Fátima apparition affirming?" And if the apparition at Fátima wanted to lead us to Jesus, I ask, "To which Jesus would the apparition lead us?" We have already reviewed the teachings of the apparitions which call for repeated daily sacrifices in reparation for the sin of the world, and wearing the

---

[236] *Blue Army Cell Manual*, pg. 5

Scapular and praying the Rosary to guarantee salvation. But if Jesus made the only Sacrifice necessary, why preach a gospel requiring many sacrifices, instead of preaching the Gospel which was given to us, requiring only One? But the apparitions want to lead us to the wrong Jesus — a weak Jesus who is still suffering on the cross and needs his mother's help to get people into Heaven.

As you will recall, the apparition of St. Michael the Archangel which preceded the Marian apparitions at Fátima gave communion to the children there. He bowed before the Eucharist to worship it and taught them to pray the following prayer:

> "Most Holy Trinity, Father, Son, Holy Spirit, I adore You profoundly and offer You the most precious Body, Blood, Soul and Divinity of Jesus Christ, present in all the tabernacles of the earth, in reparation for the outrages, sacrileges, and indifference with which He Himself is offended."[237]

And when Sister Agnes Sasagawa first began to have apparitions, they were initiated by several visions of angels adoring the Eucharist within the tabernacle at the church,[238] suggesting that Sister Sasagawa ought to do the same. This is consistent with the teachings of almost every apparition to date. They all desire to see more people worshipping the sacred bread and wine of the altar, bread and wine which is purported to become the True Body, Blood, Soul and Divinity of Jesus Christ and offered to God as a sacrifice in reparation for sins.

I will not take anyone to issue on whether the Eucharist is worthy of adoration, or whether the True Presence of Jesus is in the Eucharist at all. This book was not written to address those issues. However, if the Jesus who is present in the Eucharist is "being sacrificed at every instant on all the altars of the world" in reparation for sins committed against the Immaculate Heart of Mary, as the apparition taught Sister Sasagawa,[239] then the Jesus in the Eucharist isn't the Jesus I trusted in for my salvation. If the Jesus in the Eucharist is being offered up repeatedly to pay for

---

[237] Walsh, *Our Lady of Fátima*, pp. 41-2

[238] "Marian Apparitions of the 20th Century: A Message of Urgency"

[239] *Our Lady Queen of Peace*, "Church Approves Messages, Weeping Statue as Supernatural," pg. 16. Message of July 6, 1973. Used by permission

sins, then it isn't the Jesus of the Bible. The Jesus I trusted as Savior in 1984 paid for my sins against *Him*, and He did so only *once* — at Calvary. Jesus has no need to submit Himself again to the sacrifice of the cross as the apparitions assert, because after His payment on the cross, there is no further offering for sin.*

And since Jesus offered one Sacrifice and that Sacrifice is complete *and* sufficient, one has to wonder why the apparition teaches Theresa Lopez of Denver that "Every day," God "sends His Son to the mystery of the cross."[240] One has to wonder why the apparition tells Sister Sasagawa of Akita that the Jesus in the Eucharist is still being offered up as a sacrifice to appease the anger of God.[241] And why does the Jesus of the apparitions at Conyers teach Nancy Fowler that he is continually being offered up in the Sacrifice of the Mass in reparation for the sin of the world,[242] when the Holy Spirit, Whom the True Jesus sent to us at Pentecost, inspired the author of Hebrews to write precisely the opposite? And why does the apparition of Mary keep telling me to worship the Eucharist if it does not contain the Jesus of the Bible?

> "Jesus, the Eucharist! It is His living and true body; adore it and love it."[243]

It is this false Jesus which is offered up in the Sacrifice of the Mass, a sacrifice which can never take away sins. Notice in the daily Order of the Mass that even though the Scriptures teach that Jesus' sacrifice is finished and is complete, the priest, after changing the bread and wine into the Body, Blood, Soul and Divinity of Jesus, asks God once again to accept the Sacrifice of Christ on the altar of Heaven:

> "We...offer to you, God of glory and majesty, this holy and perfect sacrifice... Look with favor on these

---

* Hebrews 10:12-18

[240] Kuntz, pg. 59. Message of October 7, 1991

[241] *Our Lady Queen of Peace*, "Church Approves Messages, Weeping Statue as Supernatural," pg. 16. Message of August 3, 1973. Used by permission

[242] *To Bear Witness*, pg. 101, para. 176. Message of April 16, 1991

[243] *Our Lady Queen of Peace*, "An Urgent Appeal: Our Lady in Argentina," pg. 7. Message of June 1, 1986. Used by permission

offerings and accept them... Almighty God, we pray
that your angel may take this sacrifice to your altar in
heaven. Then, as we receive from this altar the sacred
body and blood of your Son, let us be filled with every
grace and blessing."[244]

As I said before, I did not write this book to criticize any
Catholic doctrines or to attack Catholics for the manner in which
they choose to honor Christ's command to 'this do in remem-
brance of me.'[245] What I wish to demonstrate here is that the
apparition of Mary, the apparition of Jesus and the apparition of
St. Michael are instructing people all over the world to offer up
more sacrifices to pay for sin as if Christ's payment on the cross
was insufficient. And it is this Sacrifice of the Mass that they are
requesting.

Which means that in lavishing its affection on the apparitions
of Mary, in bestowing riches on the shrines and statues of Mary,
by emphasizing the ritual wearing of the Scapular and praying of
the Rosary, both of which were instituted by apparitions; the
papacy, whether knowing it or not, has made itself a co-
conspirator in a worldwide effort to deceive people into trusting
that a false Jesus, or Mary, can save them. And in cooperating
with the apparition to confer the messianic attributes of Jesus
Christ on Mary, the papacy, whether inadvertently or otherwise,
has joined its hands with a spirit which preaches that a false Jesus
can take away people's sins through repeated, daily sacrifices—a
concept with which the Holy Spirit disagrees categorically, and a
ritual which was done away with completely at the institution of
the New Covenant.*

And if the apparitions of Mary, of Jesus and of St. Michael
are guilty of deception and teaching a false gospel to the masses,
then the papacy, in propagating the messages, rituals and
doctrines of the apparitions, has made itself guilty as well.

By association.

---

[244] *Sunday Missal Prayerbook and Hymnal for 1994*, "Eucharistic
Prayer Number 1," (NY: Catholic Book Publishing Company, ©1993)
pg. 27
[245] Luke 22:19b
* Hebrews 8:7-13

Secrets

> Instead of the thorn shall come up the fir tree, and
> instead of the brier shall come up the myrtle tree:
> and it shall be to the LORD for a name, for an
> everlasting sign that shall not be cut off.
> —*Isaiah 55:13*

I promised myself that this would be the shortest chapter of the book, and I intend to keep that promise. It seems that in many places where the apparition of Mary occurs, the miracles and healings are also accompanied by secrets—secrets given to the visionaries to be announced at certain dates in the future. Nancy Fowler has received some secrets at Conyers. Lucia Abóbora received several secrets at Fátima,[246] while in Medjugorje, the visionaries have received ten secrets. At Sabana Grande, Puerto Rico, the visionary Juan Angel Collado received seven secrets in 1953, three of which have been revealed, and the other four are to remain undisclosed until certain prophecies are fulfilled.[247]

On one occasion, the apparition told Mirjana Dragicevic, of Medjugorje, that the eighth secret, a coming worldwide punishment, had been reduced or softened because of the prayers and fasting of the faithful,[248] and on another occasion, Mirjana was told that the seventh secret, or chastisement, had been eliminated altogether.[249] While some of the secrets involve

---

[246] Walsh, *Our Lady of Fátima*, pp. 69n, 70

[247] *Our Lady Queen of Peace*, "Our Lady of the Rosary in Puerto Rico," pg. 13

[248] *Words From Heaven*, pg. 106. Message of November 6, 1982

[249] *Words From Heaven*, pg. 108

worldwide chastisements, others involve the occurrence of a
'Lasting Sign,' for which the video, "Medjugorje: The Lasting
Sign," receives its name. As I mentioned before, both Medjugorje
and Garabandal received promises of a 'Lasting Sign,' which
allegedly will appear at the original site of each of the apparitions
on a date that has yet to be revealed. A similar promise regarding
such a sign was made to the Denver, Colorado visionary.

I realize that some Christians may not feel comfortable with
the whole notion of the secrets, and quite frankly, neither do I.
Didn't Jesus instruct His disciples to shout out loud from the
rooftops the things He had told them in private?* But on the other
hand, Jesus often instructed His disciples not to mention to
anyone that He was the Messiah, or that He had performed a
cure,† so it might be difficult to construct a 'no secrets allowed'
type of rebuttal to the apparitions.

But if we worry about whether or not it is theologically
correct for the apparitions to tell secrets, we may miss the point of
the secrets in the first place. For my part, I am not completely
convinced that any of the secrets will take place, or that any of
them have, but even if they do, it doesn't matter to me. Does the
apparition have secrets to tell? I don't want them. One thing that it
hasn't kept secret is that it is preaching a false gospel, which is
enough for me to know to stay away. Even doves know to stay
away from their predators.

Does the apparition prophesy a lasting sign? I don't need it. I
already have one: Jesus, a lasting, imperishable sign of God's
undying love for me and for all His children. Because of Adam's
sin, thorns and thistles grew from the ground.§ Because of Jesus'
righteousness, the fir tree and the myrtle have risen to take their
place. This is the only lasting sign I need.

And whether the secrets actually come to pass or not is
immaterial. Scripture informs me that a fulfilled prophecy is no
concern to me when the prophet behind it is false. It is written,

> "And the sign or the wonder come to pass, whereof he
> spake unto thee, saying, Let us go after other gods,
> which thou hast not known, and let us serve them;

---

* Matthew 10:27

† See, among others, Matthew 17:9 and Matthew 9:30

§ Genesis 3:18

> Thou shalt not hearken unto the words of that prophet,
> or that dreamer of dreams."[250]

The prophecies and secrets of the apparitions are given specifically to keep people's attention focused on the wrong things, to keep them away from the Word, and to cause them to follow after and serve a spirit of falsehood. A miraculous sign or a fulfilled prophecy is of no consequence then, for they are given to deceive. The disciples, too, wanted Jesus to give them a secret about the end of the world, but He denied their request. Instead of giving them a secret, He told them, "Take heed that no man deceive you."[251]

Do you want to know the secrets of the apparitions? Do you want to know when the chastisements will fall? If you do, then Jesus has some advice for you:

"Take heed that no man deceive you."

Do you know how to keep yourself from being deceived? Get to know Jesus. Get to know the Word Incarnate. Read Him, study Him, eat His Word daily for your food, and wear His Word as a garment around your heart.

Then you will be fully protected.

---

[250] Deuteronomy 13:2-4a
[251] Matthew 24:4b

Epilogue

Ho, every one that thirsteth,
   come ye to the waters,
And he that hath no money;
   come ye, buy, and eat;
Yea, come, buy wine and milk without
   money and without price.
Wherefore do ye spend money for that
   which is not bread? and your labour for
   that which satisfieth not?...
Incline your ear, and come unto me: hear,
   and your soul shall live.
                 —*Isaiah 55:1-3*

WHEN writing something of this nature, it is difficult to direct the flow of thought and the presentation in a manner that will prevent anyone from taking offense. I once listened to an evangelist speak, and every night he warned the audience, "If you take offense to what I'm saying, then you're stealing, because you're taking something I'm not giving to you." That always kept the crowd humored at least for the first few minutes of his sermons, but it rarely kept anyone from taking offense once he started getting into the controversial parts of his exposition for that evening. What he said could have been considered offensive by some, and whether they were stealing or not was quite beside the point—they were offended and would not return for his service the next evening.

And I really don't think there was anything he could have done to make the content of his speeches any more palatable to his audience; he just had to plod on and accept the fact that, more often than not, there would be a different crowd the next evening and the few return customers probably would not bring anyone new with them. But he kept on, never once diluting his messages,

160

and finally left town when his seminar was complete, no more popular on his departure than he had been on his arrival.

Nonetheless, I myself have wondered how I could make this message more palatable to my target audience, that is, devotees of the apparitions—Protestant, Catholic or otherwise—but I really can't think of a way to do it. After all, the gospel the apparitions are teaching is just very, very different than the pure and simple Gospel given to the Church in the Bible. I really can't water down the issue and ultimately, if one's eternal salvation depends on the choice between the two gospels, then I really don't believe I would want to. I surely wouldn't be doing anyone any favors to pretend that the decision between the two is not a matter of Life and Death. It is.

I do believe that I could have concentrated on the more positive messages of the apparitions, though; i.e., those that could be universally supported from the Word of God. But to what end? To make one's journey into hell all the more comfortable? To justify the messages from hell itself? That's asking quite a lot.

But there really are what could be called 'good' messages. For every apparition message I recorded in Part II, there are literally thousands of others that really have nothing controversial in them at all, and I could certainly write a lengthy book about them. I could write about all the times that the apparitions of Mary request that families pray together, study the Bible together, fast, attend church and obey the Church hierarchy. Some people have written books on exactly that. There are hundreds of messages that suggest so frequently that the followers of the apparition fast and pray, that I am put to shame by the infrequent emphasis placed on prayer and fasting by Protestants, and by my own failure to do so as well.

But these 'good' messages cannot in any way excuse the falsehood that the apparitions are teaching. For example, one of the Medjugorje messages from the apparition of Mary was simply, "There is only one mediator between God and man, and it is Jesus Christ."[252] True enough. Taken by itself that message leaves me with nothing to argue about. But how can I take the apparition of Mary seriously when only a few years later at the same location it would say, 'I will intercede for you in front of God,' or in Montichiari, Italy, 'I have placed myself as the

---

[252] *Words From Heaven*, pg. 75. Message of October 7, 1981

mediatrix between my Divine Son and mankind, especially for the souls consecrated to God'?

And how should I respond to the apparition of Mary at Medjugorje when it says, "Jesus prefers that you address yourselves directly to Him rather than through an intermediary," when in the next sentence, I am told that,

> "In the meantime, if you wish to give yourselves completely to God and if you wish that I be your protector, then confide to me all your intentions, your fasts, and your sacrifices so that I can dispose of them according to the will of God."[253]

What shall I make of an apparition that wishes to lead me back to Jesus, yet gives me the option of not being so led and trusting in her instead—if that's what I want? Jesus does not wish for there to be a mediator between Himself and me, but has provided me the option of having one if I prefer? The inconsistencies are difficult to reconcile, and the matter is not made any clearer by the messages at Conyers, Georgia, where I am told, allegedly by Jesus Himself, that 'I want you, dear children, to come through My Mother on your journey back to Me.' And regardless of whether or not the apparition truly wants to convince people to go directly to Jesus, or through Mary first, its most devoted followers just go through Mary.

So while it is true that the apparitions occasionally give messages that seem to be in agreement with the Gospel, these messages are laced with serious error in intercessory theology. And the fruits of its messages are rarely, if ever, in accordance with the true Gospel anyway, which makes the frequent seemingly Biblical messages immaterial. Because even if I were to hear a thousand times over that I should trust in Jesus Christ alone, how many times would I have to hear "but trust in me, too," before I begin to wonder, "In which Jesus am I being asked to trust?" And from what Paul wrote in 2 Corinthians 11:4, we know it is possible for someone to preach a Jesus that isn't the One we received, and a gospel which is not the Truth, by a spirit which is not the One we believed.

---

[253] *Words From Heaven*, pg. 105. Message of September 4, 1982

But there is only one True Jesus and only one True Gospel and only one True Spirit, and all three of Them can be found without ever bringing the apparitions of Mary into the picture. All three of Them can be found apart from Mary, or anything that claims to be her. All three of Them can be found in the Bible.

But the millions of pilgrims who travel to Medjugorje, Conyers, Lourdes, Fátima and all of the other apparition sites, do not seem to be looking there. They return from their pilgrimages with such a lack of understanding about what the message of the Bible is and what its message offers, with no understanding that eternal life is free. Absolutely free. Through Christ alone. For example, when a group of pilgrims from Birmingham, Alabama was given the opportunity to have a question and answer session with Vicka Ivankovic, one of the Medjugorje visionaries, they asked her,

> "When Jesus promises us eternal life, does that mean eternal life in Heaven with Him, or could it be someplace else?"

and another asked her,

> "How she knows the Holy Spirit? And how one can get to know the Holy Spirit better?"[254]

Granted, these are questions worth asking, yet after these pilgrims had spent thousands of dollars on journeys to Medjugorje to ask about eternal life, nobody bothered to inform them that they could have found the answers to these questions in the Bible. For free. Instead, they are hearing the Gospel of Mary.

The apparition at Medjugorje—among many other places—has indeed spoken of its own plan to save mankind. For example, after the apparition at Medjugorje said that "God has chosen each of you, in order to use you in a great plan for the salvation of mankind," the devotees responded by saying they believe that "Medjugorje is the implementation of this plan,"[255] with no mention of Christ's death at Calvary, where God's plan was *finished*. And even though the apparition tells its followers to

---

[254] Both quotes from "Medjugorje: The Lasting Sign"
[255] *Medjugorje: The Fulfillment of All Marian Apparitions?* pg. 11

study the Bible, it reassures them that it has already secured a place for them in Heaven. So why should anyone care what the Bible says about God's plan for eternal life if the apparition of Mary has one of its own?

In this context, the omission of the true Gospel from the messages of the apparitions of Mary is most striking, and the consistency with which the apparitions avoid the concept of the Sufficiency of Christ's death is remarkable. Nothing made that more obvious to me than when Father Tomislav Vlasic interviewed Medjugorje visionary Mirjana Dragicevic after she had been receiving apparitions for 18 months and felt that she knew the Blessed Virgin Mary "very well." An excerpt of the interview follows:

> **Mirjana Dragicevic:** She also emphasized the failings of religious people, especially in small villages—for examples, here in Medjugorje, where there is separation from Serbians (i.e., Serbian Orthodox) and Moslems. This separation is not good. The Madonna always stresses that there is but one God, and that people have enforced unnatural separation.

> **Father Tomislav Vlasic:** What, then, is the role of Jesus Christ, if the Moslem religion is a good religion?

> **Mirjana:** We did not discuss that. She merely explained, and deplored the lack of religious unity, 'especially in the villages.' She said that everyone's religion should be respected, and, of course, one's own.[256]

Now I don't want to split hairs, but I would really like to know exactly what role Jesus Christ *does* play in salvation if all religions are good religions, and why it is that the apparition of Mary is so conspicuously silent on this particular issue. One of the more recent messages from the apparition of Mary was a promise that it would protect anyone who was willing to brave the Yugoslavian civil war to go on pilgrimage to Medjugorje, and that

---

[256] Weible, Wayne, *Miracle at Medjugorje: A series of columns on a modern-day supernatural religious event*, "Part 3: Interviews With The Seers," pg. 3, from an article published December 18, 1985. Parentheses and quotation marks in original

it would escort them straight to Heaven at the time of death. With assurances like that, it was no wonder that several people who were at the meeting when it was announced began to dance with joy at the thought of it, since many of them had been planning a pilgrimage themselves.* With assurances like that, it is no wonder that the Gospel of Jesus Christ is a completely foreign concept to those who follow the apparitions.

And it is no wonder that they would be offended by what I've written, because what I've written tells them to walk away from what, by all appearances, looks like Heaven's gate. What I've written tells them to walk away from what appears to be a valid source of salvation. Asking anyone to walk away from this would deeply offend them, but if I chose not to offend, I would have to avoid the true Gospel completely to do so. That is something I am not willing to do.

But like most people, I do not enjoy giving offense, so it was a difficult decision to pursue the task of writing this book. The difficulty could be substantial, which is why I discussed the issue of pursuing publication with so many of my friends before I finally went through with it. And when I had just about convinced myself not to publish, I presented the following three reasons to my friends: 1) Catholics would be so offended by this book that they wouldn't get through the first chapter, so there would be no valid reason for writing it in the first place, 2) Protestants either, a) haven't heard of the apparitions of Mary or, b) if they have, don't want to tread on the thin ice of already poor ecumenical relations by discussing the topic, and 3) those who think all things are relative and that people should believe 'whatever works for you,' would already be of the persuasion that I had found what 'works for me' and would be happy for me but disinterested in the topic.

If these three reasons were correct, then I thought there really was no good reason and no valid target group for whom to write. So for whom did I write such a book? My friends were quick to remind me that they did not fall into any of the three categories listed and were, to say the least, a little miffed that I had not provided them a category of their own. "What about the people

---

* The author, as part of his research, occasionally attends such meetings as these and was present when the announcement was made. The meeting, however, was not at a site of apparitions.

who are interested in the topic but don't have enough information to make a decision on the matter?" In other words, "What about us? Aren't we worth writing the book for?" And indeed you are.

It was one such friend who told me about the Larry King Live talk show on which Billy Graham was a guest in July of 1991. Mr. Graham had just returned from the former Soviet Union where he had been on a Crusade, and one of the listeners called in to ask him,

> "Sir, what is your opinion of the apparitions of the Virgin Mary, Mother of Jesus, in Eastern Europe for the last, I think, 13 or 14 years that the BBC has documented and so forth? What role do you think that these apparitions have played, or are playing, in the downfall of communism there?"

I am sure Mr. Graham was caught off guard by the question, but he seemed to take it in stride anyway. He responded:

> "I don't have any answer because I don't know. I've heard about it, have not investigated them, and feel that the Soviet people—the Russian people, especially, the Russian part of the Soviet Union—has always been deeply religious."[257]

So in answering the question, he actually left it unanswered, and I don't know if he did so to keep from offending the Catholic audience, or if he just didn't know what to say. But the talk show convinced me of at least one thing: there are many, many people out there who don't know the first thing about the apparitions of Mary, and who haven't had the time to study them.

So I have decided to write this for you—for all the pastors out there who preach from the Bible as the perfect, inspired Word of God, in whose care have been placed the very sheep that the apparition would like to add to its fold. For you, who have been

---

[257] Both quotes from *Larry King Live*, Host: Larry King, air date July 16, 1991 under the title, "Reverend Billy Graham: Back From the USSR; The Continuing Mystery of the Black Dahlia; Sonny Bono: And the Beat Goes On," transcript #344, pg. 5. ©1991, Cable News Network, Inc. All Rights Reserved. Transcribed by Lois Washington for Journal Graphics, Inc.

entrusted by God to prevent the deception of false gospels and counterfeit messiahs from influencing the elect. And for you, who just haven't heard and want to make a Biblical decision about whether to follow the apparitions or not.

I hope this will save you time, will keep you from having to study the apparitions at length and will save you the energy required to keep track of the many new ones that seem to occur every year. I hope, at the very least, that this will enable you to be attentive to the Word and to prayer so that you and your flock may stand strong against the schemes of the evil one.

Please tell your sheep to beware the apparition, and tell those who have succumbed to its hypnotically repetitive messages that there is Someone Who can set them free. Someone Who rescued me, and Who can rescue them, too.

Please tell them that the apparition of Mary and its cohorts are not at all who they claim to be.

Tell them that Jesus Christ *is*.

Appendix:

The Mythology of Modern Marianism

> Wheresoever this gospel shall be preached
> throughout the whole world, this also that she hath
> done shall be spoken of for a memorial of her.
> —*Mark 14:9*

IT MAY come as a surprise to some that there is a woman in the New Testament whose name will forever be linked to the preaching of the Gospel of Christ. Her name is Mary. According to the plain teaching of Christ, we shall always and forever attach her name and her obedience to the preaching of His Gospel wherever it is taught. Yes. Mary:

> "Verily I say unto you, Wheresoever this gospel shall
> be preached throughout the whole world, this also that
> she hath done shall be spoken of for a memorial of
> her."[258]

Of course, the Mary of whom Christ speaks here is not His mother. He was actually speaking of a demoniac, an indiscriminate woman of ill repute and shoddy morals, a woman who was the incarnation of impurity, once inhabited by seven devils. Now it may be hard for some to accept that Christ actually favored this

---

[258]Mark 14:9

known sinner over His own mother, but all the indications are that this is precisely what He did. Not that His selection of Mary Magdalene for this rather remarkable honor was an immediate insult to His mother, but the simple fact is that Christ's mother was passed over for it. Jesus had plenty of opportunity to finally and permanently associate His mother's name with the preaching of the Good News. He passed up the opportunity, and that more than once. Instead, He gave the honor to a simple woman whose sins had been many, frequent, and public.

One may object to this by citing Luke 1:48 where Mary declares, "behold, from henceforth all generations shall call me blessed." But the observations are first, that Mary says this of herself, and second that it has nothing to do with the *preaching* of the Gospel. Many people in all generations are blessed, but only one has the honor of being mentioned wherever the Gospel is preached. Indeed, such an honor as having the preaching of the Gospel of Christ always and forever attended by the mention of her name was reserved for Mary Magdalene *alone*.

I belabor this specific point because of the striking contrast it offers to the typical Marian apologetics of our day. In response to an earlier edition of this book, I received a letter from a Roman Catholic woman complaining that writing *Quite Contrary* was an act of disobedience to the clear teachings of the Bible:

> "Luke 1:48 expounds the Magnificat and there is no excuse for anyone claiming the name Christian to fail to carry out her scriptural mandate of, '...Behold, henceforth all generations shall call me blessed.' There is no exemption on this for any generation of Christians to not actively do so. Those journeying to approved apparition sites certainly are doing it. You are not. Who is the Bible Christian?"

I have no doubt that this woman intended by her letter to share the gospel with me and bring me into the light. What was curiously missing from her letter, however, was any mention at all of Mary Magdalene. In a letter which seemed to be written for the purpose of chastising disobedience to the Bible, I was being told to honor Mary by taking a pilgrimage to an apparition site which is nowhere commanded in Scripture. Likewise, in the same letter no mention was made of Mary Magdalene, which in fact *is* prescribed in the Scriptures. However much the apparitionists may appeal to Luke 1:48, their clear (and blatant) disobedience to Mark 14:9 reveals that being bound to the simple teachings of the Bible was never their real intention. Rather, Luke 1:48 merely provides the excuse necessary to carry on the wrongful devotion.

Scott Hahn, a Roman Catholic apologist, formerly Protestant, has likewise constructed an interesting (and fallacious) argument for his devotion to Mary. He writes,

> "First, you know that, as a man, Christ fulfilled God's law perfectly, including the commandment to honor his father and mother. The Hebrew word for honor, *kabodah*, literally means 'to glorify.' So Christ didn't just honor his heavenly Father; he also perfectly honored his earthly mother, Mary, by bestowing his own divine glory upon her. The second principle is even easier: the imitation of Christ. So, we simply imitate Christ not just by honoring our own mothers but also by honoring whomever he honors—and with the same honor that he bestows."[259]

This citation is most notable for its last sentence: "So, we simply honor Christ... by honoring whomever he honors." But nowhere in his book, *Rome, Sweet Home*, from which this selection was taken, is Mary Magdalene even mentioned. This is not to suggest that Christians should preach the Gospel of Mary Magdalene, but rather to demonstrate something that completely undoes all of Rome's arguments for the veneration of Mary. If Scott Hahn, or any Roman Catholic for that matter, truly wanted to honor Christ "by honoring whomever he honors—and with the same honor that he bestows," shrines to Mary Magdalene and books about her would so issue forth from Rome as to pile up to the heavens. If Rome wants to honor Christ "by honoring whomever he honors," then let the stampede of Magdalenian devotion begin. We do not expect to hear the hoofbeats anytime soon, because Roman Catholics honor Christ's mother for different reasons than Hahn has suggested. This is not said to make fun of the beliefs of Marian devotees, but to bring to light the fact that the arguments for Marian devotion fall apart when applied objectively and taken to their own logical ends. Roman Catholics

---

[259] Hahn, Scott & Kimberly, *Rome Sweet Home: Our Journey to Catholicism*, (San Francisco: Ignatius Press, ©1993), pp. 68-9

need to know this, and they need to know this from the Word. Only then will *both* Mary's be truly—and properly—honored.

"Fittingness"

There is no doubt that any number of falsehoods could arise out of what man thinks to be appropriate, or "fitting." The person of Mary has suffered a great many indignities due to what men have thought to be fitting. Three examples will suffice.

When Pope Pius IX proclaimed in 1854 that Mary had been conceived immaculately, without the stain of sin, he declared it to be true because it was "fitting":

> "And indeed it was wholly *fitting* that so wonderful a mother should be ever resplendent with the glory of most sublime holiness and so completely free from all taint of original sin that she would triumph utterly over the ancient serpent. ...In fact, it was quite *fitting* that, as the Only-Begotten has a Father in heaven, whom the Seraphim extol as thrice holy, so he should have a Mother on earth who would never be without the splendor of holiness."[260]

And when Pope Pius XII proclaimed in 1950 that Mary had been assumed body and soul into heaven, he declared that it was "fitting" that it should be so:

> "It was *fitting* that she who had seen her Son upon the Cross and who had thereby received into her heart the sword of sorrow which she had escaped in the act of giving birth to Him should look upon Him as He sits with the Father."[261]

And when John Paul II declared in 1997 that Mary, the mother of Christ, was the first to encounter Him when He rose from the dead, he declared it to be so because it was "fitting":

> "This year he [John Paul II] concluded a series of 50 Wednesday-noon addresses on various aspects of

---

[260] Pope Pius IX, *Ineffabilis Deus*, December 8, 1854, emphasis added
[261] Pope Pius XII, *Munificentissimus Deus*, AAS 42(1950):761, emphasis added

> Mariology, including one in May in which he went well beyond the silence of Scripture to claim that Mary was the first to experience the Risen Christ at Easter. It was, he said, only 'fitting.'"[262]

Such a statement is a plain contradiction of the truth of the Word of God which withholds that specific honor from Christ's mother, and reserves it for, of all people, Mary Magdalene:

> "Now when Jesus was risen early the first day of the week, he appeared first to Mary Magdalene, out of whom he had cast seven devils."

The problem with these arguments—aside from the obvious fact that the doctrines and assertions they support are found nowhere in the Scriptures—is that man is no judge of what is "fitting." In fact, Christ settles the dispute once and for all when He declares that what man thinks to be "fitting" God holds to be contemptible:

> "That which is highly esteemed among men is abomination in the sight of God."[263]

Or, in the charming candor of the Roman Catholic *New American Bible,*

> "What man thinks important, God holds in contempt."

The reason such matters are worthy of consideration is that if one were for a moment to apply Rome's logic, one would conclude that it was only "fitting" that Christ's gospel should ever and always be associated with a woman of purity, honor and dignity. But that is not what Christ did. No, what Christ did would be considered most "unfitting" in the eyes of men. But God holds such opinions in contempt.

"Queen Mary"

Another argument for the veneration and elevation of Mary is that her role as Queen Mother was prefigured in the Old

---

[262] *Newsweek*, August 25, 1997, Volume CXXX, No. 8, "Hail Mary," by Kenneth L. Woodward, pp. 49-55
[263] Luke 16:15

Testament. The argument stems from 1 Kings 2:19 when Solomon, the King of Israel, placed his mother on a throne and worshipped her:

> "Bathsheba therefore went unto king Solomon, to speak unto him for Adonijah. And the king rose up to meet her, and bowed himself unto her, and sat down on his throne, and caused a seat to be set for the king's mother; and she sat on his right hand."

Based on this verse, the conclusion is drawn that if the Queen Mother of the Old Testament was worthy of such honor, how much moreso the "sinless" Queen Mother of the New Testament? *Rome, Sweet Home* provides us the reasoning:

> "Mary's title as Queen of Heaven did not come from being married to God—as I had thought—but was based on the honor of being the Queen Mother of Jesus, the King of Kings and the Son of David. In the Old Testament, King Solomon, the son of David, elevated his mother, Bathsheba, to a throne at his right hand, paying her homage in his court as the queen mother. And in the New Testament, Jesus elevated his mother, the Blessed Virgin Mary, to a throne at his right hand in heaven, bidding us to pay her homage as the Queen Mother of heaven."[264]

What we notice first is the lack of any evidence from the Scripture that Jesus "elevated his mother, bidding us to pay her homage" in the New Testament. Again, though this may seem "fitting" to man, Hahn's conclusions on this matter—that Jesus elevated His mother to such a position—are contemptible to God. But there is another matter that is completely ignored in Hahn's analysis of 1 Kings 2:19—the issue of Adonijah. The context of 1 Kings 2:19 is that Adonijah, fearing the King's wrath, opts to present a request to him through his mother.* Though Bathsheba, the queen mother, obliges Adonijah this request, king Solomon reacts in the most surprising manner: he grows angry with

---

[264] Hahn, pp. 143-4
* 1 Kings 2:13

Adonijah and puts him to death.† Far from being a proof text for Marian devotion, we see a greater conflict which the Hahns opted to ignore. If the Marian enthusiast would use this passage as proof of Mary's mediating role between us and Christ, or if an apparitionist would use it to prove Mary's queenship, then they must also take with it the very conclusion that devastates their form of veneration. If this passage provides a "figure" for Mary's queenship and mediation, then it also provides a "figure" for those who would presume to approach Christ through his mother: death. That conclusion would be indeed, more "fitting."

"Just Pointing to Jesus"

Many apparition proponents contend that through her various visions, Mary is doing no more than what she did in John 2:5 at the wedding at Cana, where she tells the servants, "Whatsoever he saith unto you, do it." Presumably, these many apparitions have come to deliver to the world the same message that Mary spoke at the wedding at Cana, her last recorded statement. She desires, they assert, only to point us to Jesus. One letter which took issue with *Quite Contrary* stated, "She [the Mary of the apparitions] always points us to Her son, begs us to return to Him, and says to us the same as she said in her last recorded words in Scripture: 'Do whatever He tells you,'" while another critic added that the fact that the apparitions lead people to Christ "is dramatically testified to by the millions of people being led to the cross of Christ by Mary and other apparitions." A brief recounting of the teachings of the apparitions of Mary will disprove this.

Lucia Abóbora, the approved Fátima visionary, received in 1917 a message from 'Mary' stating, "Jesus wishes to make use of you to have me acknowledged and loved. He wishes to establish in the world devotion to My Immaculate Heart."[265] Such statements must be a cause for concern: When the apparition states that Jesus wishes to establish worldwide devotion to Mary, to whom are people being led? Later, Lucia reported that she had received a message from Jesus stating that Lucia was indeed to establish and propagate devotion to 'his mother's' Immaculate

---

† 1 Kings 2:23-25
265 Walsh, pg. 68

Heart.[266] In light of such a statement, to whom are these millions of people being led, when 'Jesus' is encouraging devotion to Mary's 'immaculate heart'?

The apparition of Mary at LaSalette, France, an approved Roman Catholic apparition stated, "For a long time I have suffered for you; if I do not want my son to abandon you, I am forced to pray to him myself without ceasing. You pay no heed. However much you would do, you could never recompense the pain I have taken for you."[267] Two questions come to mind: Why, if Mary is in Heaven where pain is no more,* is she still suffering? And by whose sufferings are Christians redeemed, Jesus' or Mary's? Scripture teaches that it was through Christ's sufferings that Christians are reconciled to God:

> "For it pleased the Father that in him should all fulness
> dwell; And, having made peace through the blood of
> his cross, by him to reconcile all things unto himself;
> by him, I say, whether they be things in earth, or
> things in heaven."[268]

Why would the apparition complain of the pain 'she' has taken for us? Was it not Christ who bore the burden of our iniquities? Was it not Christ who was pierced for our offenses, and crushed for our sins?† Yet the apparition of Mary at LaSalette seemed content to focus on 'her' sufferings, and the apparition of Mary at Fátima seemed content to focus on devotion to 'her' heart rather than pointing to Christ, as the apparition proponents insist that 'she' does. It is worthwhile to compare the teachings of this Jesus of the apparitions, a Jesus who wants to "establish through-out the world a devotion to Mary's Immaculate Heart," with the Jesus of the Scriptures Who drew public attention away from His mother at every turn.

When the crowd announced to Him that His mother was waiting for Him, He put them off and said,

---

[266] Abóbora, Lucia, *Fatima In Lucia's Own Words: Sister Lucia's Memoirs*, Kondor, Louis, SVD, ed., (Still River, MA: The Ravengate Press, ©1976) pg. 195

[267] Zimdars-Swartz, pg. 30. Message of September 19, 1846

* Revelation 21:4

[268] Colossians 1:19-20

† Isaiah 53:5

> "Who is my mother, or my brethren? And he looked
> round about on them which sat about him, and said,
> Behold my mother and my brethren! For whosoever
> shall do the will of God, the same is my brother, and
> my sister, and mother."[269]

And when a Marian enthusiast, wishing to call unwarranted attention to the womb that bore Christ and the breasts that nursed Him, interrupted Him during a sermon, Christ put off the woman's misdirected enthusiasm and stated,

> "Yea rather, blessed are they that hear the word of
> God, and keep it."[270]

If anything, Jesus' statements either elevate us to the level of Mary, or they dramatically deflate the unscriptural attempts to magnify she who was content only to magnify her God and Savior.[†] If Jesus did not exalt his mother during His earthly ministry, it certainly wasn't for lack of opportunity. The Jesus and Mary of the Bible point to Jesus. But the Jesus and Mary of the apparitions point to Mary. The inevitable conclusion is that the Jesus and Mary of the apparitions were not present at the wedding at Cana. And they are most certainly not "just pointing to Jesus."

"Gospel Confusion"

As a final note, it should be made clear, as it was in the body of *Quite Contrary*, that the apparitions of Mary fail on many points, but none so critical as the Gospel of Jesus Christ. Here, as it was earlier asserted, the apparitions of Mary fail miserably.

In the popular video called "Marian Apparitions of the 20th Century: A Message of Urgency," the viewer is instructed by the apparition of Mary at Garabandal that it is very important to deal seriously with one's sins. The viewer is told that the Lord is very offended by the sins of men and the cup of God's wrath is filled up and is overflowing. The video, an historical compilation of many Marian apparitions—approved and otherwise—takes the

---

[269] Mark 3:33-35
[270] Luke 11:28
[†] Luke 1:46-47

viewer through a series of urgent requests that we make reparation to God. Then comes the instruction from the apparition by which all of the apparitions and associated practices must be judged:

> "You should turn the wrath of God away from your-
> selves by your efforts... I ask you to amend your
> lives... You should make more sacrifices."[271]

This encapsulizes everything that is wrong with the teachings of the apparitions of Mary. Turning the wrath of God away from ourselves by our efforts is not the Gospel—*it is the very reason the Gospel is needed*. It is precisely because *we cannot turn the wrath of God away from ourselves by our efforts* that Christ died in the place of sinners and satisfied the righteous requirements of the Law for them. Jeremiah 2:22 reminds us just how futile it is to suggest that we turn the wrath of God away from ourselves by our efforts:

> "For though thou wash thee with nitre, and take thee
> much soap, yet thine iniquity is marked before me,
> saith the Lord God."

This verse also reveals for us just how hopeless the gospel of the apparitions of Mary truly is.

Another apparition of Mary, that of Medjugorje, Bosnia, contributes to this gospel confusion by making the following statement:

> "Dear children, this evening I pray that you especially
> venerate the Heart of my Son, Jesus. Make reparation
> for the wound inflicted on the Heart of My Son. That
> Heart is offended by all kinds of sin."[272]

The reason this statement by the apparition of Mary is so damaging to the Gospel of Christ is that it portrays Christ's sufferings as the cause of our separation from God when in fact

---

[271]"Marian Apparitions of the 20th Century: A Message of Urgency," Message of June 18, 1965
[272] *Words From Heaven*, pg. 162. Message of April 5, 1985

Christ's sufferings are the cause of our reconciliation. As it was written in Isaiah 53:11, God contemplated Christ's sufferings and was satisfied:

> "He shall see of the travail of his soul, *and shall be satisfied:* by his knowledge shall my righteous servant justify many; *for he shall bear their iniquities.*"

We are informed by Paul in Romans 5:1 that the reason "we have peace with God through our Lord Jesus Christ," is that Christ's sufferings *removed the offense*. They completely atoned for our guilt and satisfied the wrath of God, for Christ in His sufferings bore the iniquities of "the many." God, in Christ, punished our iniquities and thereby removed the offense by which His children were separated from Him. What is more, the Scriptures teach us that the Lord did not do this reluctantly. Rather, it was pleasing to Him:

> "Yet it *pleased* the LORD to bruise him; he hath put him to grief: when thou shalt make his soul an offering for sin..."[273]

The Scriptures teach us that the sufferings of Christ removed the offense that separated us from God. The apparition of Mary says exactly the opposite. As the citation above demonstrates, the vision of Mary at Medjugorje teaches that the sufferings of Christ *are* the offense: "Make reparation for the wound inflicted on the Heart of My Son." A testimony to the absolutely confusing and hopeless gospel of the apparitions of Mary is the fact that they assert that we need to make reparations to God for the wounds inflicted on His Son. The truth is that the wounds inflicted on Christ are the reason we do not need to make reparations!

> "Now where remission of these is, there is no more offering for sin."[274]

Leave it to the apparitions of Mary to so confuse the Gospel as to state *as the offense* the very sufferings which removed it.

---

[273] Isaiah 53:10
[274] Hebrews 10:18

"Frankly Forgiven"

In Luke chapter 7, when Simon the Pharisee was critical of Mary Magdalene's exuberance in worshipping Christ, Jesus used the occasion to teach in the form of a parable. Simon, a self-proclaimed "keeper of the law," a pharisee, could only wonder at Mary Magdalene's affection for Christ and her contrition for her sins. But Christ did not wonder at all. He said,

> "There was a certain creditor which had two debtors: the one owed five hundred pence, and the other fifty. And when they had nothing to pay, he frankly forgave them both. Tell me therefore, which of them will love him most? Simon answered and said, I suppose that he, to whom he forgave most. And he said unto him, Thou hast rightly judged."

It is interesting to see in this parable that the creditor saw what Simon the Pharisee could not: the two debtors had nothing with which to pay off their debt. The reason Simon objected to the whole scene was that he could never grasp the concept of *not* having anything with which to repay. He could only hope to appear before God one day and offer his works and his efforts as a payment against his sin debt.

But Mary Magdalene was not the least bit confused about this. She knew she had nothing with which to repay. And Christ, seeing that she came completely empty-handed, "frankly forgave" her. As the parable goes on, Christ explains that the reason Mary loved Him so much was because she had been forgiven so much. And it was through faith, not through remorse or her future good works, that she was saved.

I end on this because my devotion to God once centered on my ability to repay my debt. And my devotion centered on the mother of Christ, because it seemed "fitting." But I have since come to see that if God acted based on what *man* thought "fitting," no one would ever be saved. We are all so utterly depraved and offensive to God in our sins that for Him to save only one of us would seem "unfitting." Indeed, had that been the case, it, too, would have been "unfitting" for Christ to associate with Mary Magdalene, much less to save her. But save her, He did. And save me, He did.

In addition to the many letters I have received in criticism of *Quite Contrary*, I have also received a good number of letters and phone calls from families who are deeply concerned for their loved ones who have wandered after the visions of Mary. For many, that is the very first experience they have with regard to apparitions and they often feel helpless in their ignorance of the manifestations. Aside from the comfort they receive merely from talking about their situation, there is yet another comfort which I offer them. And if the reader finds that he or she also has close relatives and loved ones who are pursuing the visions of Mary, this comfort is offered to you as well. The comfort with which they are comforted is this: that I, too, once firmly believed in these apparitions of Mary. I, too, once seemed quite beyond salvation, absolutely steeped in the Marian dogmas of Rome. I had wandered after these deceiving spirits.

And yet, here I am, "frankly forgiven." If there is anything that I want the families of apparitionists to know it is that there was once a man who was lost in his sins, blinded to his own need for a savior, and trusting in Mary to do for him what only Christ could do. That man now writes to you that though he was lost, now he is found. So, while we are about the business of dispelling myths surrounding devotion to Mary, let us also dispel the myth that some of the Marian devotees are beyond reach. They are not. Christ *will* seek His own, and He will find them. He found me when I seemed "unfindable," and He found Mary Magdalene. He can find your loved ones, too.

Postscript

To the reader:

If after reading this you realize that you have never trusted Jesus Christ and His payment for your sins on the cross, or you realize that you have been trusting in the wrong "Jesus," I invite you to place your trust in Him, the True Jesus, now. His gift of eternal life is free. It is everlasting. By simple faith, all of Christ's righteousness will be bestowed on you as a child of God. Consider the following prayer: "Jesus, thank you for rescuing me from my sin and for granting me the free gift of eternal life. Amen." He has purposed to bring you to this point, and His Word will surely guide you from here. Please get involved in a Bible study, or find a local congregation that teaches from the Bible as the perfect, inspired, and sufficient Word of God.

To the followers of the apparition:

I invite you to reconsider the apparitions of Mary as I have—not based on feelings and emotions, as they can be misleading, but based on the Bible. Measure the apparitions against the absolute certainty of God's Word. If Mary was being impersonated, she would certainly be disheartened that you had been misled by something that wasn't even her. She would want you to test the apparitions against the True Gospel found in the Bible. She would want you to trust in Jesus Christ *alone,* and not in anything that you—or she—had done. Pray through Christ alone to God to ask

Him for guidance. If you seek Him with your whole heart, you will find Him. That's His promise, not mine.*

To the visionaries:

I invite you to read 1 John 4:2,3 and test the apparition of Mary in the manner prescribed there. The apparition has requested frequently that you test it, and this test is sure, since it is given in the Bible. And if the apparition should evade the question, ask it again, and request a Yes or No answer. Surely the apparitions will not mind being asked such a simple question, and neither should they mind providing a simple answer. Your deep desire to seek God through Jesus Christ alone will be richly rewarded. And Mary wouldn't have it any other way.

---

* Deuteronomy 4:29

Bibliography

A Call to Peace, published by MIR-A-CALL Center, Bella Vista, Arkansas, Michael Cain, editor (newspaper)

Abóbora, Lucia, *Fatima In Lucia's Own Words: Sister Lucia's Memoirs*, Kondor, Louis, SVD, ed., (Still River, MA: The Ravengate Press, ©1976)

Agnellet, Michel, *I Accept These Facts*, (London: Max Parrish and Co. Ltd., ©1958) Trans. by John Dingle from the original *Cent Ans de Miracles a Lourdes*

Aradi, Zsolt, *Shrines to Our Lady Around the World*, (New York: Farrar, Straus and Young, ©1954)

Ashley, Benedict M., O.P., *The Dominicans,* (Collegeville, Minnesota: The Liturgical Press, ©1990)

Ashton, Joan, *The People's Madonna,* (London: Harper-Collins Publishers, ©1991)

Augustine, St., Bishop of Hippo, *De Natura et Gratia*, 36, 42

Ball, Ann, *A Litany of Mary*, (Huntington, IN: Our Sunday Visitor Publishing Division, Our Sunday Visitor, Inc., ©1988)

"Betania: Land of Grace," a video narrated by Ricardo Montalban. Directed, written and produced by Drew J. Mariani, Marian Communications, Ltd., ©1993

"Between Heaven and Earth," an audio tape of the Medjugorje story, produced and directed by Caritas of Birmingham TLM Ministries, tape #4404, ©1991, all rights reserved

Blue Army Cell Manual, ©AMI Press, Blue Army of Our Lady of Fátima, Washington, New Jersey 07882

Caritas of Birmingham, quarterly newsletters, ©1991 Caritas of Birmingham

Cranston, Ruth, *The Miracle of Lourdes*, (New York: Doubleday & Company, Inc., ©1955, 1983, 1988)

Cruz, Joan Carroll, *Prayers and Heavenly Promises Compiled from Approved Sources*, (Rockford, IL: TAN Books and Publishers, ©1990)

de Montfort, St. Louis, *The Secret of the Rosary*, (NY: Montfort Publications, ©1965-92), trans. Mary Barbour, T.O.P.

Doheny, William J., C.S.C., J.U.D., and Kelly, Joseph P., S.T.D., *Papal Documents on Mary*, (Milwaukee: The Bruce Publishing Company, ©1954)

Dreams, Visions & Prophecies of Don Bosco, Brown, Eugene M., editor, (New Rochelle, NY: Don Bosco Publications, ©1986)

Duggan, Paul E., *The Assumption Dogma: Some Reactions and Ecumenical Implications in the Thought of English-Speaking Theologians*, (Dayton, OH: International Marian Research Institute, ©1989)

Geraldo, Host: Geraldo Rivera, air date December 20, 1991 under the title, "Do You Believe in Miracles?" transcript #1112. Transcribed by Journal Graphics, Inc., ©1991 by the Investigative News Group, Inc.

Graham, Anna, *Diary of a Pilgrim to Medjugorje*, December 4, 1988, not copyrighted

Haffert, John M., *Russia Will Be Converted*, (Washington, NJ: AMI International Press, ©1950)

Hahn, Scott & Kimberly, *Rome Sweet Home: Our Journey to Catholicism*, (San Francisco: Ignatius Press, ©1993)

Hasler, August Bernhard, *How the Pope Became Infallible: Pius IX and the Politics of Persuasion*, (New York: Doubleday & Company, Inc., ©1981)

Hardon, John A., S.J., *Modern Catholic Dictionary*, (Garden City, NY: Doubleday & Company, ©1980)

Holy Love: Messages from Our Blessed Mother Leading Souls to Holiness, (Seven Hills, OH: Holy Love Ministries, ©1994)

Journal of Reported Teachings and Messages of Our Lord and Our Loving Mother at Conyers, Georgia, compiled by Our Loving Mother's Children, P.O. Box 309, Conyers, GA, 30207 (newsletter)

Kuntz, J. Gary, *Our Holy Mother of Virtues: Messages for the Harvest*, vol. 1, (Denver, CO: Colorado MIR Center, ©1992)

Larry King Live, Host: Larry King, air date July 16, 1991 under the title, "Reverend Billy Graham: Back From the USSR; The Continuing Mystery of the Black Dahlia; Sonny Bono: And the Beat Goes On," transcript #344. Transcribed by Journal Graphics, Inc., ©1991, Cable News Network, Inc., all rights reserved

Laurentin, René, and Henri Joyeux, *Scientific & Medical Studies on the Apparitions at Medjugorje*, (Dublin, Ireland: Veritas Publications, ©1987)

Lord, Bob & Penny, *The Many Faces of Mary: A Love Story*, (Westlake Village, CA: Journeys of Faith, ©1987)

"Marian Apparitions of the 20th Century: A Message of Urgency," a video narrated by Ricardo Montalban. Produced and written by

Drew J. Mariani and Anne McGeehan-McGlone. Directed by Drew J. Mariani. Produced at The Eternal Word Television Network, Birmingham, AL. Marian Communications, Ltd., ©1991, International Copyrights Reserved

Macfarlane, Bud, Sr., M.I., of the Mary Foundation, Box 614, Lakewood, OH, 44107. Two speeches entitled, "Marian Apparitions Explained," on May 18, 1991 at St. Leo's Catholic Church, Elmwood, NJ and "Update on Marian Apparitions," on March 25, 1992 at Sacred Heart Catholic Church, Wadsworth, OH

Marnham, Patrick, *Lourdes: A Modern Pilgrimage*, (New York: Coward, McCann & Geoghegan, Inc., ©1981)

Mary of Agreda, *Mystical City of God: The Divine History and Life of the Virgin Mother of God: from the Immaculate Conception to the Coronation*, 4 vols. (Hammond, IN: W. B. Conkey Company, ©1914) translated from the original authorized Spanish edition by Fiscar Marison

Medjugorje: The Fulfillment of All Marian Apparitions?, (Birmingham, AL: Saint James Publishing Company, ©1991) (pamphlet)

"Medjugorje: The Lasting Sign," a video narrated by Martin Sheen. Directed by Rob Wallace, Produced by Cinematic Visions, Inc., ©1989, All Rights Reserved

Michaelsen, Johanna, *The Beautiful Side of Evil*, (Eugene, Oregon: Harvest House Publishers, ©1982)

Miravalle, Mark I., S.T.D., *Mary: Coredemptrix, Mediatrix, Advocate*, (Santa Barbara, CA: Queenship Publishing, ©1993)

Mir Response, The, published by the MIR Group, New Orleans, LA, 70151, Mimi Kelly, editor

Neuner, Josef, S. J. & Roos, Heinrich, S.F., *The Teaching of the Catholic Church*, (New York: The Mercier Press, ©1967)

Newsweek, August 25, 1997, Volume CXXX, No. 8, "Hail Mary," by Kenneth L. Woodward, pp. 49-55

1993 Catholic Almanac, Felician A. Roy, ed., (Huntington, IN: Our Sunday Visitor Publishing Division, Our Sunday Visitor, Inc., ©1992)

O'Carroll, Michael, CSSp, *Medjugorje: Facts, Documents, Theology*, (Dublin, Ireland: Veritas Publications, ©1989)

Our Lady of Fatima's Peace Plan from Heaven, (Rockford, IL: TAN Books and Publishers, Inc., ©1983)

Our Lady Queen of Peace, Special Edition I, 2nd printing, Winter 1992, Dr. Thomas Petrisko, ed. Pittsburgh Center for Peace, McKees Rocks, PA, 15136 (newspaper)

Sanchez-Ventura y Pascual, F., *The Apparitions of Garabandal*, (MI: San Miguel Publishing Co., ©1966)

Signs of the Times, published by Signs of the Times, Sterling, Virginia, Maureen Flynn, editor.

Sunday Missal Prayerbook and Hymnal for 1994, (NY: Catholic Book Publishing Company, ©1993)

"Testimony of Lylan Mitchell, The, " a video from the 1991 Marian Medjugorje Conference in New Orleans, LA, USA

To Bear Witness that I Am the Living Son of God, Vol. 1, Reported Teachings and Messages to the World from Our Lord and Our Loving Mother, compiled by "Our Loving Mother's Children," (Our Loving Mother's Children, P.O. Box 675, Newington, VA, 22122, ©1991)

Understanding Our Lady's Messages, (Birmingham, AL: Saint James Publishing Company, ©1991) (pamphlet)

Virgin Wholly Marvelous: Praises of Our Lady from the Popes, Councils, Saints, and Doctors of the Church, Peter Brookby, ed., (Cambridge, England: The Ravengate Press, ©1981)

Walsh, William J., *Apparitions and Shrines of Heaven's Bright Queen*, 4 vols., (New York: T. J. Carey, ©1904)

Walsh, William Thomas, *Our Lady of Fátima*, (New York: Doubleday & Company, Inc., ©1947, 1954)

Weible, Wayne, *Miracle at Medjugorje: A series of columns on a modern-day supernatural event*, "Part 3: Interviews With The Seers"

Words from Heaven: Messages of Our Lady from Medjugorje, 5th ed., (Birmingham, AL: Saint James Publishing Company, ©1991)

Zimdars-Swartz, Sandra L., *Encountering Mary*, (New York: Princeton University Press, Avon Books, ©1991)

Glossary

Adoration of the Wafer (see Eucharistic Adoration)

Alb (see also Stole): Part of the outer dressing of a priest. It is worn like a robe.

Altar boy: A young boy, usually of middle school to high school age, who assists the priest at the altar during the Sacrifice of the Mass.

Altar: The 'table' at the front of a Catholic Church. The altar is where the Sacrifice of the Mass is offered in reparation for the sin of the world.

Apocryphal: A term defining a writing, declaration or document that is considered by Church scholars to be sacred or honorable, but lacking canonicity.

Apparition: A visual supernatural encounter.

Assumption: The doctrine that was proclaimed by Pope Pius XII in 1950, declaring that Mary had been taken up, body and soul, into Heaven upon the completion of her earthly ministry.

Ave Maria: Latin for the prayer 'Hail Mary.' (See page 19)

Benediction: A ritual during which a consecrated wafer is placed upon the altar for adoration and meditation.

Blessed objects: Any medal, crucifix, religious article or pendant that has been blessed by a priest, or by the apparition of the Virgin Mary.

Bishop: A member of the Church hierarchy. Above a priest, but below an archbishop or a cardinal.

Brother: A title given to a male member of a religious order.

Brown Scapular (see Scapular, Brown)

Bull, Papal: As in "bulletin." An official document issued by the pope.

Cardinal: A member of the Church hierarchy. Above an archbishop but below the pope.

Cardinal Legate: A member of the College of Cardinals who is sent as a vicarious delegate by the pope.

Caritas of Birmingham: An organization dedicated exclusively to the worldwide distribution of the messages from the apparition of Mary at Medjugorje, Bosnia.

Caritas: A Latin wording meaning 'Love.'

Centenary: A celebration honoring the 100-year anniversary of an important event.

Co-redemptress (see also Redemptress): A title given to Mary with the understanding that she works in cooperation with Christ to bear the burden of the sin of the world.

College of Cardinals: Hand picked members of the pope's advisory council.

Communion, Sacrament of: One of two sacraments initiated by Jesus Christ. The other sacrament is Baptism. Christians celebrate communion to honor Christ by partaking of bread and wine in memory of His death on the cross. In Catholicism, the bread and wine are believed to be the True Presence of Christ—that is, the bread really is His flesh, and the wine really is His blood.

Confession, Sacrament of: One of the sacraments instituted by the Catholic Church, whereby a sinner confesses sins and obtains absolution, or cleansing of those sins, from God, through the mediation of a priest.

Consecrated: A term describing the wine and host, or bread, that have been through the process of transubstantiation by a priest, and are therefore considered to be the True Presence of Jesus Christ in the form of real flesh and real blood.

Coronation (of Mary) (see also Mysteries, Rosary): The last of the five Glorious Mysteries of the Rosary. It refers to the belief that Mary, upon her ascension into Heaven, was crowned Queen of Heaven and Earth.

Corruption: Bodily decay in the grave. This is in reference to the belief that Mary's body did not undergo corruption in the tomb. This belief was necessitated by the Immaculate Conception dogma, and was used as a premise for the Assumption dogma.

Crucifix: A cross with an image of Christ affixed to it.

Dance of the Sun (see Miracle of the Sun)

Decade (see also Rosary, Mystery, Glory Be): Ten "Hail Marys," a "Glory Be" and an "Our Father," make one decade. A complete Rosary is prayed by reciting one decade for each mystery, of which there are 15.

Diocese (see also Parish): A term used to define a geographic boundary within the Catholic Church. A diocese is to an archdiocese much like a county is to a state.

Ecstasy: A term used to describe the state of extreme happiness and satisfaction that visionaries experience during an apparition, inner locution or other form of paranormal interaction with the apparition of Mary.

Eucharist (see Communion, Sacrament of)

Eucharistic Adoration: Time spent on one's knees in front of a consecrated host, or wafer, in reverence and adoration as if it were truly Jesus Christ, Himself.

ex cathedra: Literally, "From the Chair." That is, the Chair of St. Peter. When a pope speaks with respect to the definition of an article of Christian faith, he speaks *ex cathedra*. It is held among Catholics that when the pope speaks *ex cathedra*, he cannot err.

Exterior locution (see Outer Locution)

Feast Day: A special day during the Church calendar year set aside for prayer about, and meditation on, a Church-centered event in history. For example, the Feast of the Assumption is celebrated on August 15 of every year.

fides catholica: Obligatory faith. A matter of doctrine which those who deny, cannot legitimately be called Catholics. The Assumption dogma is a matter of *fides catholica,* or Obligatory faith.

fides humana: Non-obligatory faith, or human faith. A matter of doctrine which is acceptable to the Catholic Church, but is not required of Catholics. Belief in the apparitions of Mary is a matter of *fides humana.*

Glory Be (see also Rosary, Decade): One of the minor prayers of the Rosary: "Glory be to the Father, to the Son and to the Holy Spirit. As it was in the beginning, is now, and ever shall be, world without end. Amen." It is recited after the completion of one Our Father and ten Hail Marys.

Holy Father: Another name for the pope.

Holy water: Water that has been blessed by a priest. In Catholic circles, the use of holy water is frequently prescribed as a method of discerning spirits.

Homily: The time during the Sacrifice of the Mass when the priest preaches about the Bible reading for that day.

Host: Another term for a Communion wafer, or Eucharistic wafer.

Imaginative vision: A paranormal experience during which the recipient experiences images that are familiar and which infuse wisdom.

Immaculate Conception: The doctrine that was proclaimed by Pope Pius IX in 1854, declaring that Mary had been conceived without sin, that is, immaculately, and was therefore born outside of the bloodline of Adam.

Immaculate Heart of Mary: Usually pictured as a heart pierced by a sword, in reference to Simeon's prophecy in Luke 2:35.

Ineffabilis Deus: The Papal Bull (1854) in which Pope Pius IX declared that the Immaculate Conception was a divinely revealed doctrine of the Catholic faith.

Infallibility (see also, *ex cathedra*): The belief that the pope, when speaking *ex cathedra*, cannot err.

Inner Locution: A paranormal experience during which the recipient hears a voice, but not through the physical ear.

Intellectual vision: A paranormal experience during which the recipient suddenly feels the strength and direction needed to accomplish a substantial task. Intellectual visions are not necessarily accompanied by visual stimulation.

Interior locution (see Inner Locution)

Jesuit: The Order of the Society of Jesus. Members belong to one of three levels of the society: the solemnly professed, the spiritual coadjutors, or the lay brothers. Founded by Ignatius Loyola in 1540, the Jesuits boast the largest membership of any Catholic order.

Lasting Sign (see also Secrets): The promise of the apparition to provide a Lasting Sign at the site of an apparition. A Lasting Sign was promised at the site of the Medjugorje apparitions, as well as those at Garabandal, Spain and Denver, Colorado, USA.

Lenten season, or Lent: A forty day period preceding the celebration of Easter Sunday during which something (e.g., a bad habit or certain food item) is given up, or sacrificed, in reparation for sins.

Marian Year: One Church calendar year that is dedicated, by papal proclamation, to be a time of honoring Mary.

Mass (see Sacrifice of the Mass)

Mediatrix: A title given to Mary with the understanding that she mediates between God and man, or between Jesus and man.

Miracle of the Sun: A phenomenon that accompanies many Marian apparitions. Eyewitnesses claim that they see the sun spinning, changing to all colors of the rainbow, and then plummeting to earth and rising again. Less dramatic accounts at various apparition sites still describe the changing colors and the distinct appearance that the sun is getting closer, then farther away.

Miraculous Medal: A medal given to Saint Catherine Labouré by an apparition of Mary. On the front, it is stamped with an image of Mary with the words, "O, Mary, conceived without sin, pray for us who have recourse to thee." On the back is an image of the Immaculate Heart of Mary alongside the Sacred Heart of Jesus, surrounded by twelve stars (see back cover).

Monastery: A religious, single sex, communal living environment.

Monsignor: A title given to a priest by the pope, giving him an elevated dignity or distinction.

Munificentissimus Deus: The Apostolic Constitution (1950) in which Pope Pius XII declared that the Assumption of Mary was a divinely revealed doctrine of the Catholic faith.

Mysteries , Joyful (5) (see also Rosary, Decade): Each of the Joyful Mysteries represents a meditation on an event for one decade of the Rosary, that is, for ten Hail Marys. The five Joyful Mysteries are: The Annunciation to Mary, the Visitation of Mary, the Nativity, the Presentation in the Temple, and the Finding of Jesus in the Temple.

Mysteries, Sorrowful (5) (see also Rosary, Decade): Each of the Sorrowful Mysteries represents a meditation on an event for one decade of the Rosary, that is, for ten Hail Marys. The five Sorrowful Mysteries are: The Agony in the Garden, the Scourging at the Pillar, the Crowning with Thorns, the Carrying of the Cross, and the Crucifixion.

Mysteries, Glorious (5) (see also Rosary, Decade): Each of the Glorious Mysteries represents a meditation on an event for one decade of the Rosary, that is, for ten Hail Marys. The five Glorious Mysteries are: The Resurrection, the Ascension of Jesus, the Descent of the Holy Spirit, the Assumption of Mary, and the Coronation of Mary as Queen of Heaven and Earth.

Mystical City of God: A four volume work subtitled, *The Divine History and Life of the Virgin Mother of God: from the Immaculate Conception to the Coronation.* It comprises the entire recorded revelation of the apparition of Mary to Sister Mary of Agreda, Spain *circa* 1617.

Neck (of the Body of Christ): A name referring to Mary. It stems from the belief that she is above the Body proper, but below Christ, the Head, and actually joins to two.

Obligatory Faith (see *fides catholica*)

Ordinary: A bishop with special jurisdiction over a Diocese. The ordinary oversees all of the bishops of a diocese.

Our Holy Father: Another name for the pope.

Outer locution: A paranormal experience during which the recipient experiences a real stimulation of the ear.

Papal Bull (see Bull, Papal)

Parish (see also Diocese): A Catholic congregation. A parish is to a diocese as a city is to a county.

Parochial school: An elementary, middle, junior high or high school that is supported and operated by a local Catholic parish or diocese.

Parturition: Childbirth.

Paten: A plate that is held under a consecrated host to prevent crumbs from falling on the ground while the wafer is being placed on the tongue or in the hands of the recipient.

Phenomenon of the Sun (see Miracle of the Sun)

Pilgrim: Someone who journeys to the site of an apparition.

Pilgrimage: A pious endeavor to visit a shrine or site of an apparition.

Priest: A Catholic clergyman. Only a priest can perform the process of transubstantiation, hear confessions, and administer the other sacraments of the Church.

Purgatory: A Catholic belief in a place between Heaven and hell where sinners, through punishments, pay off the balance of the price for their sin before entering into Heaven. It is held that souls in purgatory can obtain earlier entrance into Heaven if they, while living, were devoted to Mary through the Rosary and the Brown Scapular, or through the Sacrifice of the Mass, or both.

Redemptress (see also Co-redemptress): A title given to Mary with the understanding that she suffers in order to redeem sinful man by paying a portion of the price for sin.

Roman Pontiff: Another name for the pope.

Rosary (see also Glory Be, Decade, Mysteries): A method of prayer. The Rosary contains 54 beads connected in a loop which begins and ends with five beads and a crucifix (see back cover). Each bead represents a "Hail Mary" or an "Our Father." It is recited by praying one "Our Father," 10 "Hail Marys," and one "Glory Be" which makes one decade. A complete Rosary is prayed by reciting 15 "Our Fathers," 150 "Hail Marys," and 15 "Glory Be's."

Sabbatine Privilege (see also Purgatory, Scapular): A privilege granted to wearers of the scapular, whereby they are guaranteed to be escorted by Mary from Purgatory into Heaven on the first Saturday after their death.

Sacred Heart of Jesus: Usually pictured as a heart surrounded by thorns to represent the suffering of Christ on the cross.

Sacred objects (see Blessed objects)

Sacrifice of the Mass: The religious ritual during which bread and wine, having been changed into the body and blood of Christ, are offered as a sacrifice in reparation for the sin of the world.

Salve Regina: Latin for 'Saving Queen.' It is the original name for the prayer called the 'Hail Holy Queen.' (See page 75)

Scapular, Brown (see also Sabbatine Privilege): Two pieces of cloth held together by strings and worn over the shoulders so that the cloth pieces would rest simultaneously on the chest and back of the wearer (see back cover). The Brown Scapular was given to St. Simon Stock in 1251 by an apparition of Mary, with the promise that anyone who wore it would not go to hell.

Secrets (see also Lasting Sign): Apparitions of Mary usually give secrets to visionaries. The secrets contain prophecies of catastrophic future world events, or personal secrets for the benefit of the visionaries.

Sign of the Cross: Much like an 'amen,' the sign of the cross ends a prayer, or is used in blessing someone. It is done with the hand by tracing the four points of the cross either over one's own torso (forehead to chest, then shoulder to shoulder), or in front of the person being 'crossed.'

Sister: A title given to a female member of a religious order.

State of Grace: A term describing one's spiritual condition. According to Catholic doctrine, if someone dies in the State of Grace, they will gain access to Heaven based on the merit of their pious meditations or good behavior. Otherwise, time in Purgatory is required to cleanse the soul.

Stations of the Cross: A ritual during which observers meditate on each of the events that led to the crucifixion and burial of Christ, e.g., the scourging, the weeping women, the nailing to the cross, etc.

Stole (see also Alb): A long, thin article of clothing worn by a priest during the Sacrifice of the Mass. It is worn over his alb.

Sword of sorrow: The sorrow that Simeon prophesied for Mary at the presentation of Jesus in the temple (Luke 2:35).

Tabernacle: A place where something sacred is stored, usually in reference to the consecrated bread and wine. Also in reference to the messages of the apparition of Mary, as in "the Tabernacle of Our Lady's Messages."

Transubstantiation: The process by which bread and wine become the real body and blood of Jesus Christ during the Sacrifice of the Mass. Only a Catholic priest can perform transubstantiation.

Visionaries: Those who actually see apparitions or experience inner or outer locutions, and receive messages.

Wafer (see Host, Eucharist)

Subject Index

Names of visionaries and locutionists in **bold face**.

195

Scripture Index

Tim Kauffman was born in 1965 in San Diego, California, and raised in a military family. He spent his childhood traveling through and living in the states of Hawaii, California, Massachusetts, Oregon and Colorado, respectively. He received his Bachelor of Science in Mechanical Engineering from the University of Colorado at Boulder in 1989, and is now employed as an engineer with the National Aeronautics and Space Administration in Huntsville, Alabama.

what are these "Marys" teaching? Their many statements betray their origins, as Kauffman examines their words in light of the Bible to show that these apparitions are not whom they claim to be.

Formidable Truth: A Vindication of Loraine Boettner
by Robert M. Zins, Th.M., 54 p. $4.95

No Protestant scholar has come under more fire from Rome this century than Loraine Boettner, author of the exposé of Roman dogma and doctrine, *Roman Catholicism*. Zins comes to Boettner's defense to show that in spite of the many unfounded accusations of poor scholarship, Boettner still stands. *Formidable Truth* originally appeared as Appendix II in Zins' *Romanism* under the title, *Veritas Formidabilis*.

On the Edge of Apostasy: The Evangelical Romance with Rome, by Robert M. Zins, Th.M..................................$10.95

Just as Paul once asked, "...what fellowship hath righteousness with unrighteousness? and what communion hath light with darkness?" (2 Corinthians 6:14), Zins asks, "What fellowship hath Protestants with Romanists?" Knowing that Protestants and Roman Catholics adhere to two different gospels, Zins concludes that many of today's evangelicals who are increasingly complicitous with Rome are wandering dangerously close to the edge of apostasy.

(There is an additional fee to cover the expenses of shipping and handling: $3.00 per book, plus 0.50 for each additional item to the same address. See order form, facing page, for details.)

To contact White Horse Publications, please write to:

White Horse Publications
PO Box 2398
Huntsville, AL 35804-2398

or call toll free:

1-800-867-2398

White Horse Publications
http://whpub.com

Order Form

(photocopy this form and mail it with a check made payable to White Horse Publications, PO Box 2398, Huntsville, AL 35804-2398, USA)

Name _____

Address _____

_____

City _____ State _____ Zip _____

----

*Geese in their Hoods: Selected Writings on Roman
Catholicism by Charles Haddon Spurgeon*
compiled & edited by Timothy F. Kauffman, 204 p.
....$9.95 x ____qty. = _____

*Romanism: The Relentless Roman Catholic Assault
on the Gospel of Jesus Christ!*
by Robert M. Zins, Th.M., 280 p.
....$8.95 x ____qty. = _____

*Graven Bread: The Papacy, the Apparitions of Mary,
and the Worship of the Bread of the Altar*
by Timothy F. Kauffman, 206 p.
....$7.95 x ____qty. = _____

*Quite Contrary: A Biblical
Reconsideration of the Apparitions of Mary*
by Timothy F. Kauffman, 206 p.
....$7.95 x ____qty. = _____

Formidable Truth: A Vindication of Loraine Boettner
by Robert M. Zins, Th.M., 54 p.
....$4.95 x ____qty. = _____

On the Edge of Apostasy: The Evangelical Romance with Rome,
by Robert M. Zins, Th.M., 280 p.
....$10.95 x ____qty. = _____

shipping ($3.00 for one item,
plus .50 for each additional
item to the same address) ....$_____

Total...$_____
(International orders: checks must be drawn on a US Bank. *Add $5 for
shipping)*